Pie Every Day

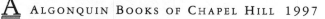

Pie Every Day

RECIPES AND SLICES OF LIFE

by PAT WILLARD

A ALGONQUIN BOOKS OF CHAPEL HILL 1997

Published by
ALGONQUIN BOOKS OF CHAPEL HILL
Post Office Box 2225
Chapel Hill, North Carolina 27515-2225

a division of
WORKMAN PUBLISHING
708 Broadway
New York, New York 10003

Printed in the United States of America.
Published simultaneously in Canada by Thomas Allen & Son Limited.
Design by Nancy Loggins Gonzalez.
Illustrations by Judy Pedersen.
Line drawings by Billy Kelly.

Grateful acknowledgment is made to the following for permission to reprint their recipes:

"Mississippi Mud Pie" from *As Easy as Pie* by Susan G. Purdy, ©1984 by Susan G. Purdy, reprinted by permission of Scribner, a division of Simon & Schuster.

"Sweet Potato Pie" from *Soul Food* by Sheila Ferguson, ©1989 by Sheila Ferguson, reprinted by permission of Grove/Atlantic, Inc.

LIBRARY OF CONGRESS CATALOGING-IN-PUBLICATION DATA
Willard, Pat.
    Pie every day : recipes and slices of life / by Pat Willard.
       p.   cm.
    ISBN 1-56512-147-3
    1. Pies.   I. Title.
TX773.W69   1997
641.8'652—dc21   96–47650
                                                      CIP

10 9 8 7 6 5 4 3 2 1
First Edition

ACKNOWLEDGMENTS

I would like to express my deep appreciation to Carl G. Sontheimer, president of the Cuisinart Cooking Club, Inc., for an afternoon of fine conversation and for granting me permission to adapt recipes from the club's magazine, *The Pleasures of Cooking*. I would also like to thank the current editors at *Farm Journal* for permission to use recipes from their 1965 cookbook, the *Complete Pie Cookbook*.

This book wouldn't have been written without my mom's good cooking skills, the years of teaching (and eating) given to me by Andy Birsh, and all the friends and relatives who gave me recipes and kindly let me stuff them with pie. For their constant support, I would especially like to thank Dan Cullen and Mary Chris Welch, Kathleen Cromwell, my sister, Sue, my brother, Joe, my editor, Shannon Ravenel, for her patient guidance through the intricacies of the English language, and finally, and very deeply, Sallie Gouverneur, who didn't laugh when I told her I'd been thinking a lot about pies.

Thank you all with love.

CONTENTS

In honor of my Pop,
John J. Willard,
and Chris's Mom,
Sally Seidman

March 1996

With love to Chris

Pie Every Day

Pies at the BarTen

To know the right woman is a liberal education.

—ELBERT HUBBARD, FROM *THE ROYCROFT DICTIONARY
AND BOOK OF EPIGRAMS*

When I got married, I moved to a small town in Ohio called Ravenna where my husband, Chris, was a reporter for the county newspaper. Before I married I was writing a novel and working as a community organizer down in Atlanta, Georgia. But afterward, when all the boxes and hand-me-down furniture were packed into the small attic rooms of our first apartment, I had to find a job. After months of applying for the few jobs that fit my background, I settled in as the morning waitress at the BarTen Restaurant. It was considered one of the best positions in town, and I got the job only because the newspaper's photographer was a favorite customer and had vouched for my worthiness. I liked the job because it rescued us financially, but more because it gave me time in the afternoons to write. My shift started at seven, when the farmers came in for eggs, and coffee fortified with whiskey, and ended shortly after two, when the county judge from the courthouse across the street finished his turtle soup.

Unlike the afternoon and evening waitresses, I was expected to do some food preparation and to help cook breakfast when Senia or Anna, the cooks (both well into their seventies), were busy preparing the day's specials. In my family, being a good cook was considered a natural part of life, so in no time I was skillfully poaching eggs, flipping hash, and folding omelets. I liked being in the kitchen early in the morning and watching the hungry men and women smelling of dirt and hay plow through the breakfasts I made for them. While Senia and Anna told me stories about their lives, I fell into the quiet, peaceful rhythm of the work. Between the good talk and the simple food we served, by the time my shift ended, I felt, on most days, ready for the writing I was doing at home. But what I really longed to do, from the first day I began at the BarTen, was to learn to make pies the way Betty made them.

Betty was the midday waitress. She arrived at ten with her husband and unmarried son trailing behind her, all bearing trays of freshly baked pies. She had the best station in the restaurant—the one in front by the bar where all the lawyers and businesspeople liked to sit. She left promptly at two, when her husband came back to pick her up. Dressed in a neat white pantsuit, her white hair a flurry of curls, Betty smoked and gossiped through the workday. A good Christian woman with a husband who had his own trucking business, she didn't much need anyone's approval. She was not well liked by the staff because she had a rigid authority about her; cool and efficient, she gave the impression that she was a waitress above the pack. Betty grew to like me despite my college degree and sometimes strange opinions, but mostly, I think, because she knew I wasn't after her son the way she was convinced the evening waitress (a tramp, if Betty ever saw one living and breathing) was. When I finally got to know her well enough to ask her how to make a pie, she chalked up my ignorance to being a young city bride and wrote down the recipe for an all-purpose crust, including as a bonus the trick for a creamy custard filling.

It was as if I had just been given the secret to a long and happy life. The recipe was written surreptitiously on the back of a check (so that the others in the kitchen wouldn't see) and slipped to me at the end of my shift while I was putting on my coat. On my way home, I stopped at the grocery store and bought lard, eggs, and cornstarch. I forgot about everything else except what I was about to do. I kept thinking about the banana cream pie I was going to present to my husband that night, envisioning the swirling mass of meringue peaks on top and my husband's blissful face when he cut into it. At a time when we were still trying to find our footing together, the idea struck me as an essential equation that went something like this:

My husband loves pies + I learn to make pies = We will be forever one

So I hugged my bags of groceries and secret recipe and hurried home. For the rest of the afternoon I worked on that pie. At first, the dough stuck to the rolling pin, but eventually I rolled it out and got it somehow into the pie plate that I had received as a wedding present but had not taken out of the box until that day. The filling thickened, the bananas were ripe. Everything, it seemed, was coming out right.

Since the filling had to sit for a few hours, I planned to put the meringue on just before dinner and let it brown while we ate. When Chris came home, he brought a few of his coworkers with him. We made a pitcher of martinis and sat out on our small roof deck. I sat there very pleased with myself and my secret, anxious for the other men to leave us alone. But another pitcher of drinks was mixed and somehow five of us sat down to eat the dinner I had prepared for Chris and me. Though I remembered to add the pie's meringue before I began serving, I forgot to take the pie out of the oven until I saw smoke pouring from the loose oven door. I ran to open it but it was too late; the meringue was a sooty mess.

This was the first important lesson I learned about pie-making—a blemished pie can almost always be salvaged. The bottom and custard were still okay, and the unsuspecting guests went on talking as I quickly spooned off some of the more burned bananas and meringue, whipped up more egg whites, and this time stood right in front of the oven window while the meringue browned lightly. I brought the pie to the table, gave the men strong cups of coffee, then cut into the pie with a knife dipped in hot water. After they took their first bite, I watched their faces melt with satisfied pleasure. When our guests finally left, the pie was nearly gone. Chris greedily scooped up the remains of the custard and broken pieces of crust from the bottom of the pie plate.

I made pie after pie after that, learning from Betty how to make a lattice top, a graham crust, gravy for savory pies. She taught me about the different types of flour and fat she used for flaky, short, and cobbler crusts. One day at the BarTen Senia overheard Betty and I talking about pies and there ensued a heated discussion about vegetable shortening versus butter. Senia was for butter and pure lard; Betty swore by Crisco. I tried both and sided with Senia that butter gives crust more taste. My choice caused a breach in my friendship with Betty for a while. It seemed that although recipes for pie crusts are fairly standard and simple, there are as many opinions about quantity and method as there are bakers in the country. Even the wife of the restaurant owner, a very regal but sickly woman named Dotty roused herself when she heard about the goings-on from her husband to come down and give her opinion. She was a peacemaker in that her sweet crust was made with margarine, which produces a substantial, but less flaky, crust.

I gradually realized that every woman in town knew how to make a pie and most could do it with their eyes closed. As far as they were concerned, I was just doing what I was supposed to as a novice wife with a hungry husband to feed and a household to run. For me, though, making pies remained simply a pleasurable way of marking time. Yet even as I smiled at the quaintness of measuring a woman's worth by the quality of her crust, I began to see a certain strength in it. Betty made her daily allotment of twelve pies while babysitting her grandson, straightening up her house, and packing a hefty lunch for her husband. She gave hardly a thought to making pies. It was just something she did along with everything else. And yet it gave her a great deal of pride and pleasure to be known for her marvelous creations. No one who ate her pies thought of them simply as desserts. Rather, her pies were recognized as a symbol of a tradition passed on from one woman to the next. When I asked her how she managed to bake a dozen pies every morning, she shrugged and looked at me as if I were truly as foolish as she thought I was, with my education and funny opinions. "There's nothing to it," she said. "You just do it."

Later that year, after my husband was accepted into graduate school, we packed up and moved to New York City. I soon found a job helping to produce a newsletter that published restaurant reviews. I took cooking lessons from some of the best chefs in the city, ate in their restaurants, and attended their lectures. Yet what I learned from them was simply a variation on what I had gathered in the kitchen of the BarTen, especially from Betty. Making different kinds of pies had taught me about sauces, spices, flours, and fats. Pies could be fancy and elegant or humble and quick; they could feed two romantic souls or a pack of wolves. What I had learned about pies stuck with me for life.

The other day my youngest son sat at the kitchen counter struggling through his homework. My other son came in for lunch, followed by one of our dogs and my husband; a football got tossed around while math questions were shouted above the barking dog and brotherly taunts. Farther down the counter, I calmly pressed the rolling pin over the top of the wax paper and concentrated on the dough spreading below the sheet. It was this, I thought, that Betty taught me. Here I was, hundreds of miles away, far from a farm and in another life, with career and family crowding in on me, and I was doing nothing more special than finding a certain bit of harmony in the making of a pie.

All Kinds of Crusts

Fear always springs from ignorance.

—RALPH WALDO EMERSON, "THE AMERICAN SCHOLAR"

I f pies could be made without crusts, more people would bake them. A good crust should be flaky, hardy enough to hold the filling, and tender enough to bite into easily. It should not intrude on the flavor of the filling, yet it should have its own subtle characteristics that complement what it is holding. Given these criteria, it's no wonder that, though composed of the simplest ingredients, a fine pie crust is considered one of the most difficult culinary feats to achieve.

And it doesn't help matters much that when you pick up a cookbook and turn to the section on pies, there is always a paragraph or two about just how hard it is. Yet in the same breath, it's intimated that all good cooks make good crusts as a matter of course.

All of which is cruel, defeating, and so untrue. Even Betty, making her dozen pies a day for the BarTen, would bring in a stinker or two. (We called them dog pies for the dog who lived in the back alley and would pull the pies from the trash and eat them.) In the time I knew her, Betty brought in pies that exemplified everything that can go wrong with a crust. There were soggy messes or pale and undercooked crusts that tasted like glue paste. Particularly memorable was the coconut cream pie that couldn't be cut. When the best kitchen knives couldn't break through the bottom crust, the filling was finally scooped out and served as pudding.

With pie crusts, even professional chefs have to admit there's a certain amount of fate and a dash of magic involved. To assure everything comes out right, the flour should be fresh, the fat chilled, and the cook should have nothing more in mind than the task at hand. Have all that and there's an even chance something will happen to spoil it—like the weather (is it humid? is it dry? is it hot?) or the phases of the moon (a proper old wife once repeated to me an old wives' tale about the hazards of mixing dough during the full moon). One time in Ohio, Chris and I were taken by the newspaper's resident gourmet and a few of his friends to what was reputed to be the finest restaurant in the central part of the state—the dining room of a Sheraton Hotel. It served very traditional haute French cuisine in a large, formal room with crystal chandeliers, uncomfortably tiny gold chairs, and a small orchestra that played dance music. We started with aperitifs and appetizers and proceeded to such entrées as beef Wellington and roast leg of veal in a truffle sauce, all accompanied by a few lovely bottles of rich red wine. The meal ended with brandy and desserts—for me a tarte Tatin and a much-needed cup of strong coffee. The chef, a tall, rotund man, dressed all in white, had been making his rounds through the dining room, but by the time he came to our table, we were just finishing dessert. He saw the remains of the apple tart on my plate and asked me why I hadn't finished it. I replied that, after such a hefty meal, I was simply full. But that wasn't good enough. He tasted the tart and exclaimed it a disaster. The apples were too sharp, and the crust, "Ach!" he said. "The crust. It's a disgrace." What did I know? It was my stomach that was aching, not my taste buds. But then he gave the reason for this perceived disaster in our midst. "Well, of course, our pastry chef is a woman and she must be ovulating." He walked away from our table, perfectly satisfied. Deeply offended by his sexist remark, I never went back to his restaurant.

And yet underneath the chef's stupid statement was a grain of truth. A good crust is something to be wondered at by man and woman, like modern-day alchemy.

People did not used to be so picky about how their crusts came out. When the first European settlers came to America, the pie recipes they brought with them called for crusts that acted as cooking pots. As dense and tasty as baked clay, the pastry that surrounded the first American pies was broken apart to get at what was inside. If it could be eaten at all, it was because the gravy and juices on the interior had softened it until it could be used like a biscuit to sop up the remains. In 1758, Dr. Acrelius, a Swedish parson visiting America, wrote back to his family that he had been served an abundance of apple pie whose crust "is not broken if a wagon wheel goes over it."

The English settlers often used suet, or solidified rendered drippings from meat, for their crusts. When baked, this kind of dough turns a wonderful golden color but is as hard as plasterboard and has a strong animal taste. My grandmother, who came to this country from Ireland, made the mistake of preparing her first American blueberry pie with a crust that was made of suet. It was winter when she started working as the cook for a wealthy family that lived in a mansion on the Main Line in Philadelphia. Every time they asked for something she had never heard of, she'd run across the lawn to the next house and ask her second cousin, who was the cook there (that's how she got her position in the first place). Cousin Mary would explain what it was they wanted her to do and Grandmom would hurry back with some semblance of a recipe in her head. But the blueberry pie was requested in the summer at the family's beach house in Cape May, New Jersey. There was no one there to ask except the parlor maid, who could only say a pie had a crust that held the berries, and some sugar should be sprinkled on top. Grandmom, who never exactly followed a recipe in her life (and never used measuring spoons, either; she used her palm, cupped tightly or loosely, depending on the measurement), thought it all sounded easy enough and proceeded to make a dough the way she would for biscuits, using chilled suet cut from the Sunday roast. The pie came out looking so beautiful, she recalled, that she insisted on serving it herself, though no one tasted it until she left the room. When the plates came back to the kitchen, the little blue wedges were almost all intact.

Grandmom was not asked to make another pie again that summer and didn't know what she had done wrong until she got back to Philadelphia and told the story to Cousin Mary. She couldn't explain the failure: the berries were fresh and sweet and she'd used the best suet. "Suet!" Mary exclaimed.

"Sure," my grandmother said. "That's what makes a pastry gold."

The idea that a pie's crust should actually taste as good as its contents took hold gradually in this country. As life in America settled down a bit and the different nationalities in the New World mingled together and added to one another's culinary repertories, crusts gradually improved. With proper kitchens set up in more permanent homes and less worry about the wolf at the door, cooks began to try to match the flavor of the crust to the richness of the meat and fruit that the countryside provided as fillings. New England cookbooks from the late eighteenth century list a number of concoctions called "turn under pies" or (even better) "humbug pies." These were, very simply, fruit sweetened with molasses and cooked in a dish covered on top by a single crust. Before it was served, the crust was cracked open and stirred into the filling. Now we call these dishes pandowdies and preparing them is a good way to practice crust-making techniques. You get the benefit of learning how to handle dough without the performance anxiety, and you still end up with a wonderful dessert!

What we have come to think of as the standard, proper crust was what our ancestors would make only on special occasions. In the past, ordinary pies, the kind that were made almost every day in kitchens across the country, were deemed successful if they did not crumble when you bit into them. Pies were often made in batches through the week and stored in pie chests—or "safes"—those now very expensive little cupboards you see in decorated "country" kitchens. Pies were the original convenience food, relied upon for a quick snack. In the BarTen, Betty and the other women cooks all said they were taught to make pies when they were as young as six years old. Except for Anna, who grew up in a small town in Italy and landed in Ohio as a war bride (only to be abandoned by her husband as soon as she arrived), they were all raised on farms where pies were eaten first thing in the morning. The members of the household grabbed slices and ate them while going about their early chores. Everybody had another slice at the midday meal and again in the afternoon as a snack, all slices washed down with coffee from a forever brewing pot. A cake might or might not be made for dessert with either lunch or dinner, but there was always pie.

This was because pies were easy to transport and because anything could be folded into a crust—seasonal fruit, preserves, custards, or leftovers. For an everyday, workhorse kind of pie, the crust had to be substantial and, to this end, most old-fashioned crust recipes called for vegetable shortening, such as Crisco, or lard. These kinds of fats make a dense crust that is, while less flaky, still delicious and easy to bite into. Denser still, but with a strong following among old pie cooks, is the hot-water crust. Contrary to everything you have ever heard about making crust, the fat in this recipe is stirred into boiling water to a creamy paste, then mixed with the flour; the result is a very strong crust, particularly good for juicy or heavy fillings.

But pies for company, for church dinners, and for town fairs were

Fats

B utter, margarine, vegetable shortening, lard, and suet are all fats used to make pie crusts. Each one plays a distinct role in the ultimate taste and flakiness of the baked crust.

BUTTER will give the richest flavor, but what you gain in taste you lose in flakiness. A butter crust is meltingly tender and firm, almost like a thin butter cookie.

MARGARINE is actually a type of vegetable shortening. To my mind, the only time margarine should be used is when you're serving someone who is watching his or her cholesterol level. If you must use it, make sure you use a solid stick, not a spread (which would be too watery and yield unsatisfactory results). Margarine produces a very malleable dough, best rolled out between wax paper. The crust will be slightly oily—not flaky—and will taste just a little better than a crust made with solid vegetable shortening.

VEGETABLE SHORTENING, such as Crisco, is used by the pie maker whose sole goal is to produce a flaky crust. A shortening crust is strong and nearly tasteless—a blessing when making pies with juicy fillings whose flavors are meant to shine alone.

LARD, rendered and clarified pork fat, produces the flakiest crust of all. Make sure you use leaf lard, which is rendered from pork kidney fat. It does not have a strong animal taste—in fact, a crust made with leaf lard is all but tasteless, yet tender and a wonderland of flakiness.

SUET is unprocessed beef fat. Some of the savory recipes that I have gathered from old cookbooks and from friends of my mom call for suet. When I make these recipes, I buy the best beef suet I can cajole out of my local butcher. A suet crust is hard—almost like a crusty biscuit—and has a slightly meaty flavor.

In sorting out which fats to use for which recipes, consider the filling. If it's very juicy, go with vegetable shortening. If you're out to impress someone with a true, flaky American pie, choose lard. And if you're like me, and have long ago assigned your cholesterol level to God's hands for the sake of enjoying life with all the good taste you can manage, then use a combination of $\frac{2}{3}$ butter to $\frac{1}{3}$ lard.

another matter altogether. In parts of the country where farm fairs and church suppers were popular, the makers of pies brought to be auctioned off or sold could be identified by the decoration on the upper crust. Local families were known by a particular way they had with spirals or an intricate weave or an extra frill around the edge or a complicated layering of decorative dough shapes. Yellowed photographs in old magazines and cookbooks show pies that look like fancy Parisian hats or witty visual puns from Marcel Duchamp.

As modern life took over, however, homemade pie production began to fall by the wayside. What I think of as the demise of the country's pie culture happened when women started to leave the home to go to work. With no more time to make a dozen workday pies, women began to replace their family's morning pie slice with packaged Danish pastry, and other sorts of convenience food began to fill in the gaps throughout the rest of the day. When the urge came on to make a pie, women now felt that their efforts had to be special, that they had to make one of those fair pies instead of a regular pie, and that's when all the crust heartaches began. Cooks had gotten out of the habit of making crusts and, when they did try, their expectations were higher than they needed to be. Manufacturers, quick to pick up on this national distress, marched in with premade pie shells and crust mixes that, while acceptable, did not erase the memories of truly delicious, homemade crust.

The solution to modern crust anxiety lies with the food processor. Crusts truly made "by hand" taste slightly more delicate, but that's almost beside the point. Given a tub of fresh-picked fruit and a certain look in my family's eyes, I'll pull out the processor any day. There's a trick to using the processor that follows closely the principle for mixing dough by hand, and no matter what the purists say, once followed the results are just as exquisite.

BY PROCESSOR. Start with everything thoroughly chilled, from the flour to the processor's work bowl and metal blade. If you think far enough ahead, put everything in the refrigerator overnight; if not, place the flour, the work bowl, and the metal blade in the freezer—$\frac{1}{2}$ hour should be sufficient. Then proceed thus:

1. Mix the dry ingredients together in the food processor by pulsing 2 or 3 times.

2. Cut the chilled fat into small pieces and scatter on top of the dry ingredients.

3. Pulse in short, quick intervals until the flour resembles cornmeal (2 or 3 pulses should do it).

4. Sprinkle the first tablespoon of cold water through the feed tube; pulse once. Add another tablespoon; pulse again. Continue until the dough *just* holds together. Turn the dough out onto a sheet of plastic wrap spread on the counter. Swiftly gather the ends of the wrap together and, as you cover the dough, form it into a slightly flattened disk. (The point here is to keep the warmth of your hands away from the dough.) Refrigerate for 30 minutes to an hour.

BY HAND. Again, everything, including the mixing bowl, should be very cold. It helps to have a pastry blender but you can also work the fat in with your fingertips. Either way, speed is of the essence.

1. Stir together the dry ingredients in a bowl.

2. Cut the fat into small pieces and quickly start mixing it with the flour until the flour resembles cornmeal.

3. Begin to sprinkle cold water, 1 tablespoon at a time, over the flour-fat mixture. As you work, push the moistened part of the mixture to one side, adding to it as the rest of the mixture becomes moist.

4. When the flour mixture just about holds together, turn it out onto a floured work surface. Knead quickly with the heel of your hand until it holds together. Shape the dough into a disk, wrap it in plastic wrap, and refrigerate for 30 minutes to an hour.

If you are really gung ho about learning about pies, use the hand method first and work your way through the crust recipes in this chapter. In addition to the basic recipes for shortening, lard, and butter crusts, I have provided several different variations—those best used for hors d'oeuvres and savory pies; crumb crusts; biscuit and mashed potato crusts—as well as the technique for handling phyllo, dumpling skins, and empanada wrappers. These recipes will teach you about the effects different fats have on flour and how even the slightest variation in procedure can change the taste and texture of your results. The winter after my second son was born I worked at home more, but I found myself caught in a strange dilemma: although I had a lot of responsibilities, I was too tired to do anything constructive. With a cranky baby in a sling or in a backpack (he was a fast grower!) and my older son and his friends close by, I began to practice making pie crusts just to keep my senses alive. I started by baking empty pie shells, then letting the older children and my husband taste-test the results before feeding what remained to the birds in the backyard. When my family got sick of eating crusts, I wrapped the empty shells up tightly and stacked them in the freezer. (They stay good for about three to four months; defrost completely before you add a filling.)

The kind of flour you use is very important. I once attended a cooking class taught by Edna Lewis, one of the best American cooks around, and she was adamant about using only Heckers brand all-purpose flour for her pies and biscuits. The reason she gave was that it has a lower gluten content than any other commercially available flour. A lower gluten content produces a very tender, flaky crust.

I know some people who order their flour by mail from specialty baking catalogs and I even know a few crazy ones who will drive for hours to a store in Lancaster, Pennsylvania, where Amish farmers sell their locally milled wheat. I don't consider either of these a suitable way to spend time or money. My suggestion is to try Heckers flour or, if it's not available in your area, test a few other brands until you find one you like. The recipes in this book were tested with all-purpose white flour. If you prefer whole wheat crusts, look for a finely milled brand (try a good health-food store) and use equal parts of whole wheat and white flour.

As you proceed with your practice crusts, pay attention to how the flour looks when the fat is cut in and then how it changes with each tablespoon of cold water. Don't worry if you need to add a few more tablespoons of water than a recipe calls for. This is part of the magic of making crusts. The amount of water depends on things you have no control over, namely the dryness of the flour and the air. Enough water has been added when the dough just holds together—it should never look moist, but there should never be bits of dough left in the bowl either (if this happens, add another tablespoon of water). When you've gotten the feel, then try the recipes with a processor, using the steps outlined on pages 13–14.

Once you've actually made the dough and chilled it properly, the next challenges to meet are rolling it out and getting it into the pan, both of which lead to rolling pins.

It's hard to talk rationally with some people about the kind of rolling pin they use. There are essentially three types of pins: the traditional wooden pin with handles that are either stationary or rotate with ball bearings; a long wooden dowel; and a pin made of marble. The kind you end up with is as personal a choice as deciding who you want to spend the rest of your life with. You can talk up the virtues of one type of pin to someone of another persuasion and, totally unswayed, the person will look at you as if you were a sideshow barker. My sister helped to roll out the recipes in this book using our grandmother's traditional wooden pin with stationary handles. Our mother used it, too, through all her years of baking, but she gave it to Sue when she decided she was finished with cooking. This was at a time when Sue was producing babies one after another and, with what was left of her enormous energy, turning every foot

Crust Troubleshooters

There are a few things you can do to minimize problems—even on your worst day:

• Chill everything—flour and bowl included—for at least 30 minutes beforehand or keep a sack of flour in the refrigerator just for pies. For a quick chill, place the flour in the bowl and throw it in the freezer for 15 minutes.

• Measure flour and fat accurately.

• Use pans with dull surfaces, such as Silverstone, glass, or ceramic, so heat isn't reflected away from the pie during baking.

• If a crust cracks while you're rolling it out, too little water was added. It's best to start over from the very beginning, but if you must use it, carefully pick it up and lay it on a cutting board; cover with a damp towel and put it back in the refrigerator for 30 minutes. The dough will be a little moister, but the baked results will suffer slightly in terms of flakiness.

• If the bottom of an uncooked crust splits before it's filled, patch it by dampening a piece of leftover crust and pressing it gently over the hole.

• If a crust shrinks, you've stretched it out too much in the pan. Always drape the walls of the pan generously with the dough (even leave it a little wrinkly) and don't pull up on the crust to flute the edges. To stop a shell from shrinking when prebaking it, cook it with another pie pan inside for 8 minutes at 450°F. Remove the top pan and continue baking for another 7 minutes or until the crust is golden brown.

• If a crust fails to brown, either you used too little fat or too much liquid or, when you rolled it out, you used too much flour. Chalk the pale crust up to experience.

of available soil around her house into vegetable and flower beds. Her small house was on the side of a steep, curving hill, and its tiny garden bumped up against a granite hillside. Across the street, in what was once the parking lot of the Josie D. Heard A.M.E. Church, she coaxed and mulched and composed the worn dirt into a field of vegetables, enough to feed her family and several other families besides.

When the fall and winter came, I'd go into Sue's tiny kitchen and find her rolling out dough for dinner with our grandmother's pin. The pies she made were stuffed with vegetables from the garden, but she also made tortes, pizzas, and thick, yeasty focaccia. She told me once that what she likes about the pin is its comfortable heaviness and its size. It's about a foot long and the handles are a bit warped at the ends where you place your fingers. Sue says it's like an extension of her arms, which is exactly how a good rolling pin should feel.

I, however, use a long (twenty-one-inch) straight wooden dowel pin that's about two inches in diameter. It's made of hard oak, just heavy enough that I don't have to exert a lot of force, and is stained a beautiful medium brown from its years of use. What I like about this type of pin is that my hands can slide easily up and down its length to concentrate pressure where the dough needs thinning. I'm not a very precise person and a rolling pin like this allows me to be a bit free with the dough. Sue rolls out perfect circles of dough. I don't and probably never will.

Marble pins come in both styles, with handles and as long cylinders without handles. Marble is good to use in the summer because its cold surface helps keep the fat from melting. But it's heavy and can be tricky to control over the surface of the dough. If you're making a lot of pies, marble can also take a toll on your arms and back. On hot summer days, I have found it better to roll out the dough on a large slab of marble that I can slip into the refrigerator for a half hour than to use a marble rolling pin. I've seen marble boards sold in cooking stores for a lot of money, but I picked up mine from a dumpster in front of a tile contractor's workshop. It's worth your while to find a local contractor of your own and cruise by to see if there are any extra pieces lying around.

Whatever type of pin you settle on, the method for rolling out the dough is the same. Place the pin in the center of the dough and roll out, either away from you or toward you. Turn the dough slightly and repeat until the dough is slightly bigger than the pan to which you're going to transfer it. Try not to labor over the rolling. Put gentle, steady pressure on the pin but don't smack the pin down on the surface of the dough. Also, pay attention to the amount of flour you sprinkle on your work surface. Too much flour could dry out the dough, causing it to toughen or crack.

When you have rolled out the dough to the desired shape and size, drape one end of it over the rolling pin and raise it from the work surface. Slide the baking pan under the hanging dough and gently lower the dough into place. Press the dough gently—and quickly— against the walls of the pan. Don't stretch the dough up the side, but allow a bit of a cushion and some overhang. Crimp the edges as you desire and proceed with the rest of the recipe.

Fancy Rims and Pretty Top Crusts

The magic of a pie is partially due to its appearance. There is nothing as charming—or I think seductive—as the sight of a pie embellished with an intricate top crust and a decorative edge. Somehow it reminds me of a little girl's dress puffed out like a tutu with a ruffled petticoat peeking out from underneath.

My pies don't often look that fine. As with any artistic endeavor, it takes time and patience to achieve a truly breathtaking pie effect. I'll do it for special occasions and for company, but a plain old fork trim or fluted edge and a top crust with maybe a funny-shaped vent is about all I can usually muster.

When I do go all out, here are some things I do.

EDGES

Unless otherwise noted, begin by folding the edge of the dough under to make a double rim around the pie.

Scallops: Pinch the pastry together between your thumb and index finger to make little loose U's around the rim of the crust. When you've gone all the way around, press a fork between the U's to flatten the pastry against the pie pan.

Rope: With your hand angled slightly away from the rim of the pie pan, pinch a little of the dough between your thumb and the first knuckle of your index finger, then press your index finger down into the depression your thumb has just made. Repeat around the edge of the crust.

Wreath: Fold the edge of the dough under so the dough is doubled and hanging slightly over the rim of the pie pan. With scissors, snip V shapes at regular intervals around the edge of the pie. Separate the top and bottom of each V shape, pushing the top V up and the bottom V down. Repeat around the rim.

Ruffles: Carefully insert a finger under the dough and lift it slightly away from the pie pan. Press the pastry on one side of the lifted portion firmly down against the pie pan. Repeat evenly around the rim.

Dots: Press the handle of a measuring cup or spoon that has a hole in it into the dough (cups or spoons that are sold together on a ring will have holes in the handles). The pastry will pop up a bit into the hole to form a small dot. Repeat around the rim of the pie.

Shapes: Trim the edge of the dough so that it is even with the pie pan. Using the leftover pastry scraps, cut out shapes using any "tools" you have on hand, such as cookie cutters, bottle caps, Play-Doh molds, etc. Moisten the pie rim with cold water and place the shapes around the rim, overlapping slightly. Press the shapes lightly into the rim.

Braid: You need a lot of scraps for this one. Trim the edge of the dough so it is even with the pie pan. Cut 3 long, $\frac{1}{2}$-inch-wide strips from pastry scraps and braid them together to form a single braid long enough to go around the rim. Moisten the pie rim with cold water and coil the braid around the rim. Tuck the ends of the braid into one another or disguise the joint by cutting out a pretty shape from scraps, moistening the bottom of the shape, and layering it over the braid's ends. Press the braid lightly into the rim.

TOPS

For a solid top crust, try one of these embellishments.

Glitter Tops: Lightly sprinkle the top crust with cold water, then dust it evenly with granulated sugar.

Shiny Tops: Brush the top crust with an egg wash made by combining 1 beaten egg yolk with 1 teaspoon cream, milk, or melted butter.

Decorative Vents: Use small cookie cutters or cut out shapes freehand with a sharp knife.

For lattice and spiral crusts, start by rolling the dough slightly thicker than usual. It will make the dough easier to handle.

Lattice: Cut strips from the dough that are about $\frac{1}{2}$ inch wide. Moisten the rim of the bottom crust with cold water and lay half the strips over the filling, about 1 inch apart. Place the remaining strips on the diagonal to create a diamond pattern. Trim the strips even with the pie edge. Turn the bottom crust over the rim and ends of the strips. Press firmly all around and flute the edges. For a fancier, rippled effect, twist each strip as you lay it across the filling.

Woven Lattice: Cut strips from the dough that are about $\frac{1}{2}$ inch wide. Moisten the rim of the bottom crust with cold water and lay half the strips across the filling. At an outer edge of the pie, weave the first cross strip through every other bottom strip. This will be your guide strip. To make the rest of the weaving go easier, fold every other bottom strip halfway back over the guide strip. Place the next strip down near the guide strip over the strips that are not folded back. Unfold the others over the new strip. Continue, alternating folding strips back as you weave across to the edge of the pan. Trim the strips even with the pie edge. Turn the bottom crust rim over the ends of the strips. Press firmly all around and flute the edges.

Spirals: Cut ½-inch-wide strips and fasten them together by moistening the ends with cold water, then pressing them together to form one long strip. Start at the rim and swirl the strip over the top of the pie (laying it down flat) to cover the filling, ending near the center. Trim the excess or let it hang down over the crust like the end of a ribbon. Turn the bottom crust up over the edge of the spiral. Press firmly to seal and flute the edges.

Dada Spirals: Here's where your imagination takes over. Cut the strips a little narrower, about ¼ inch wide, and fasten them together by moistening the ends with cold water and pressing them together to form one long strip. Start at the rim this time and work your way to the middle, just let the spiral form freely in unusual patterns. You can make it go across, then down, or back and forth in V shapes. My favorite is to take a very long strip and just keep piling the strip up over the filling to form a small funnel in the center. Decorate with any extra scraps or moisten and sprinkle with sugar to make the funnel sparkle.

THE INSTRUCTIONS FOR all but a few of the crust recipes listed here call for a food processor. If you want to make your crusts by hand, I suggest you start with the recipe for the Hot-Water Crust (page 29) or one of the two listed under "Andy's Crusts" on page 31 because they're pretty foolproof. Once you've conquered those, branch out to the other recipes using the hand method described on page 14.

Betty's Pie Crust

*T*his is the recipe Betty gave me in the kitchen of the BarTen when I first asked her about pies. It's a sturdy crust, with a subtle flavor that in no way undermines the filling.

3 cups sifted all-purpose flour, chilled
1¹/₂ teaspoons salt
1 cup good-quality vegetable shortening or lard, chilled
6 to 7 tablespoons iced water

1. In the bowl of a food processor fitted with the metal blade, pulse together the flour and salt. Cut the shortening or lard into small pieces and, with the top of the processor off, scatter over the flour mixture, then re-cover and pulse 2 or 3 times. Pour 1 tablespoon iced water down the feed tube and pulse once. Add another tablespoon and pulse. Continue adding tablespoons of iced water until the dough just holds together.

2. Turn the dough out onto a sheet of plastic wrap. As you wrap the dough in the plastic, form it into a disk. Refrigerate for 30 minutes.

3. Take the dough from the refrigerator and cut it into 2 pieces, one slightly bigger than the other. Wrap the smaller one in plastic wrap and return to the refrigerator. Roll out the bigger piece on a lightly floured surface until it's slightly larger than the pie pan. Drape one end of the dough over the pin and gently lift it up, then slip the pan underneath the dough and lower it into the pan. Press the dough gently—and quickly —against the sides of the pan. Refrigerate the crust for at least 30 minutes before either filling or prebaking (prebaking instructions are on page 28).

4. If you are making a pie with a top crust, after you have filled the pie, take the smaller disk from the refrigerator and roll it out on a lightly floured surface until it's a little bigger than the pie. Drape one end of the dough over the rolling pin, lift it gently, then drape it over the top of the filling. Press the edges together and crimp to seal. Slash a

few vents across the top of the crust to allow steam to escape and bake the pie according to the directions in the recipe you are using. (If you're not making a pie with a top crust, either freeze the second dough disk or make an extra bottom crust.)

MAKES A DOUBLE 9-INCH CRUST.

Butter and Lard Crust

*T*his crust recipe offers the best of two worlds—the flavor of butter and the strength of lard. You can use this crust for any pie recipe, but if your filling is savory rather than sweet, eliminate the sugar.

3 cups sifted all-purpose flour, chilled
¼ cup sugar (except for savory pie crusts)
Pinch of salt
8 tablespoons (1 stick) unsalted butter, chilled and cut into 8 pieces
⅓ cup lard, chilled and cut into small pieces
6 to 8 tablespoons iced water

1. Combine the flour, sugar, and salt in the bowl of a food processor fitted with the metal blade. With the top off, sprinkle the butter and lard over the dry ingredients. Re-cover and pulse a few times until small clumps form. Begin to add the iced water through the feed tube, 1 tablespoon at a time, pulsing quickly until the dough begins to form into a ball. Turn the dough out onto a sheet of plastic wrap. As you wrap the dough in the plastic, form it into a disk. Refrigerate for 30 minutes.

2. Take the dough from the refrigerator and cut it into 2 pieces, one slightly bigger than the other. Wrap the smaller piece in plastic wrap and return to the refrigerator. Roll out the bigger piece on a lightly floured surface until it's slightly larger than the

pie pan. Drape one end of the dough over the pin and gently lift it up, then slip the pan underneath the dough and lower it into the pan. Press the dough gently—and quickly—against the sides of the pan. Leave about an inch of dough hanging over the sides of the pan and cut any excess away. Refrigerate the crust for at least 30 minutes before either filling or prebaking (prebaking instructions are on page 28).

3. If you are making a pie with a top crust, after you have filled the pie, take the smaller disk from the refrigerator and roll it out on a lightly floured surface until it's a little bigger than the pie. Drape one end of the dough over the rolling pin, lift it gently, then drape it over the top of the filling. Press the edges together and crimp to seal. Slash a few vents across the top of the crust to allow steam to escape and bake the pie according to the directions in the recipe you are using. (If you are not making a pie with a top crust, either freeze the second dough disk or make an extra bottom crust.)

MAKES A DOUBLE 9-INCH CRUST.

All-Butter Crust

*T*his is the most delicious crust I make and the one I use most often. But it's a bit more delicate than other crusts and not suited to fillings with a lot of juice.

SINGLE OR DEEP-DISH 9-INCH CRUST

1½ cups sifted all-purpose flour, chilled
½ teaspoon salt
8 tablespoons (1 stick) unsalted butter, chilled and cut into 8 pieces
4 to 5 tablespoons iced water

DOUBLE 9-INCH CRUST
3 cups sifted all-purpose flour, chilled
1 teaspoon salt
14 tablespoons (1³/₄ sticks) unsalted butter, chilled and cut into 14 pieces
7 to 8 tablespoons iced water

1. In the bowl of a food processor fitted with the metal blade, pulse together the flour and salt. With the top off, scatter the pieces of butter over the flour mixture. Re-cover and pulse 2 or 3 times until the flour resembles coarse meal. Pour 1 tablespoon iced water down the feed tube and pulse once. Add another tablespoon and pulse. Continue adding tablespoons of iced water until the dough just holds together. Turn the dough out onto a sheet of plastic wrap. As you wrap the dough in the plastic, form it into a disk. Refrigerate for 30 minutes.

2. For a double-crust pie, divide the dough into 2 disks, one slightly bigger than the other. Wrap the smaller disk in plastic wrap and return it to the refrigerator until after you've filled the pie. For a single crust or the bottom of a double crust, roll out the piece of dough on a lightly floured surface until it's slightly larger than the pie pan. Drape one end of the dough over the pin and gently lift it up, then slip the pan underneath the dough and lower it into the pan. Press the dough gently—and quickly— against the sides of the pan. Leave about an inch of dough hanging over the sides of the pan and cut any excess away. Refrigerate the crust for at least 30 minutes before either filling or prebaking (prebaking instructions are on page 28)

3. If you're making a double crust, after you have filled the pie, roll out the remaining disk on a lightly floured surface. Drape one end of the dough over the rolling pin, lift it gently, then drape it over the top of the filling. Press the edges together and crimp to seal. Slash a few vents across the top of the crust to allow steam to escape and bake the pie according to the directions in the recipe you are using.

Prebaking a Pie Crust

I've come across several methods for prebaking a pie shell that are as intricate as dance steps. This is the most straightforward way I know.

1. Preheat the oven to 425°F.

2. Prick the bottom and sides of the pastry with the tines of a fork. Place a sheet of aluminum foil that is slightly bigger than the pie pan loosely inside the bottom of the pan (over the dough) and fill with pie weights. You can buy actual pie weights, but I've successfully used everything from nuts and bolts to beans and small stones.

3. Bake in the center of the oven for 10 to 12 minutes. Remove the foil and weights and return the shell to the oven.

4. Lower the heat to 350°F. For partially baked shells, bake another 3 to 5 minutes. For completely baked shells, bake for another 10 to 12 minutes. If the edges begin to brown, cover them with a strip of aluminum foil.

Hot-Water Crust

Very sturdy indeed, this crust is excellent for main dish and fruit fillings with a lot of juice in them. I've never made this crust in a food processor—though there's no reason it couldn't be done.

⅓ cup boiling water
⅔ cup vegetable shortening
1 tablespoon milk
2 cups sifted all-purpose flour
½ teaspoon salt

1. In a large bowl, pour the boiling water over the shortening and beat with an electric mixer or a fork until creamy. Add the milk and let the mixture cool. Mix the flour and salt together, then stir into the cooled liquid. You can use this dough immediately or wrap it in plastic wrap and chill. (Chilling slightly will make the rolling easier.)

2. Roll the dough out on a lightly floured surface until it's slightly larger than the pie pan. Drape one end of the dough over the pin, gently lift it up, then slip the pan underneath the dough and lower it into the pan. Press the dough gently—and quickly —against the sides of the pan. Crimp the edges as desired. Refrigerate the crust for at least 30 minutes before either filling or prebaking (prebaking instructions are on page 28).

MAKES A SINGLE 9-INCH CRUST, WITH SCRAPS LEFT OVER.

Buttermilk Crust

*T*he slightly sour taste of this crust complements many different fillings, particularly those featuring fruits and nuts.

3 cups sifted all-purpose flour, chilled
2 tablespoons sugar
8 tablespoons (1 stick) unsalted butter, chilled and cut into 8 pieces
¼ cup plus 2 tablespoons vegetable shortening,
chilled and cut into small pieces
½ cup cold buttermilk

1. In the bowl of a food processor fitted with the metal blade, pulse together the flour and sugar. With the top off, scatter the pieces of butter and shortening over the flour mixture. Re-cover and pulse a few times until the flour looks like coarse meal. Add the buttermilk and pulse 1 or 2 times until the dough begins to gather together. Turn the dough out onto a piece of plastic wrap and gather the ends together, forming the dough into a disk. Wrap with the plastic and chill for at least 30 minutes.

2. Take the dough from the refrigerator and cut it into 2 pieces, one slightly bigger than the other. Wrap the smaller piece in plastic wrap and return to the refrigerator. Roll out the bigger piece on a lightly floured surface until it's slightly larger than the pie pan. Drape one end of the dough over the pin, gently lift it up, then slip the pan underneath the dough and lower it into the pan. Press the dough gently—and quickly—against the sides of the pan. Leave about an inch of dough hanging over the sides of the pan and cut any excess away. Refrigerate the crust for at least 30 minutes before either filling or prebaking (prebaking instructions are on page 28).

3. If you are making a pie with a top crust, after you have filled the pie, take the smaller disk from the refrigerator and roll it out on a lightly floured surface until it's a little bigger than the pie. Drape one end of the dough over the rolling pin, lift it gently, then

drape it over the top of the filling. Press the edges together and crimp to seal. Slash a few vents across the top of the crust to allow steam to escape and bake the pie according to the directions in the recipe you are using. (If you are not making a pie with a top crust, either freeze the second dough disk or make an extra bottom crust.)

MAKES A DOUBLE 9-INCH CRUST.

Andy's Crusts

The following recipes come from my neighbor Andy (see "Men and Pies," page 210), who bakes a different pie nearly every Sunday. Whenever I pretend I'm visiting his wife, he pulls out his latest copies of all the new food magazines and we start doing what I really came to their house to do. We look through all the recipes, talk about techniques, and cattily critique famous cooks. We have a glass of wine and then I go home and answer my family's questions about what took me so long at Andy's house. Andy is a very handsome, robustly masculine man, and the people I live with have a hard time believing Andy really sits around exchanging recipes with me. So, more often than not, I tell them I was learning how to use something like a power saw and don't even begin to let on that the dessert we're eating is one of Andy's creations.

The recipes for both of these crusts call for the hand method (see page 14) because that's the way Andy gave them to me, and I have always followed his lead (though, of course, they can also be made in the processor). Both doughs are very strong and can withstand a certain amount of fumbling, which means they're great for crust beginners.

Spice Crust

Andy has used this crust for both pumpkin and apple fillings. He sometimes adds a half cup of walnuts—finely chopped—to the dough.

2 cups sifted all-purpose flour, chilled
$\frac{1}{2}$ teaspoon baking powder
$\frac{1}{2}$ teaspoon ground cinnamon
$\frac{1}{4}$ teaspoon ground nutmeg
$\frac{1}{4}$ teaspoon ground cloves
$\frac{1}{4}$ teaspoon salt
1 tablespoon unsalted butter, chilled
$\frac{3}{4}$ cup vegetable shortening, chilled and cut into small pieces
$\frac{3}{4}$ cup iced water

1. In a mixing bowl, combine the flour with the baking powder, spices, and salt. Cut in the butter and add the shortening, stirring with a fork just until the flour resembles coarse meal.

2. Add iced water, a little at a time, until the dough just comes together. Turn the dough out onto a piece of plastic wrap and gather the ends together, forming the dough into a disk. Wrap with the plastic and refrigerate for at least 30 minutes.

3. Divide the dough disk into 2 pieces, one slightly bigger than the other. Wrap the smaller piece in plastic wrap and return to the refrigerator. Roll out the bigger piece on a lightly floured surface until it's slightly larger than the pie pan. Drape one end of the dough over the pin and gently lift it up, then slip the pan underneath the dough and lower it into the pan. Press the dough gently—and quickly—against the sides of the pan. Leave about an inch of dough hanging over the sides of the pan and cut any excess away. Refrigerate the crust for at least 30 minutes before either filling or prebaking (prebaking instructions are on page 28).

4. If you are making a pie with a top crust, after you have filled the pie, take the smaller disk from the refrigerator and roll it out on a lightly floured surface until it's a little bigger than the pie. Drape one end of the dough over the rolling pin, lift it gently, then drape it over the top of the filling. Press the edges together and crimp to seal. Slash a few vents across the top of the crust to allow steam to escape and bake the pie according to the directions in the recipe you are using. (If you are not making a pie with a top crust, either freeze the second dough disk or make an extra bottom crust.)

MAKES A DOUBLE 9-INCH CRUST.

Lemon Crust

Andy has used this crust for all kinds of fruit fillings. I have used it for a simple custard pie and, omitting the sugar and vanilla, for the shrimp tart recipe on page 194. Andy disagrees with me on the shrimp, but try it and decide for yourself who's right.

2 cups sifted all-purpose flour, chilled

1 tablespoon unsalted butter

1 tablespoon sugar

$\frac{1}{2}$ teaspoon baking powder

$\frac{1}{2}$ teaspoon vanilla extract

$\frac{1}{4}$ teaspoon salt

Juice of 1 medium lemon

$\frac{3}{4}$ cup vegetable shortening,
chilled and cut into small pieces

$\frac{3}{4}$ cup iced water

1. Mix all of the ingredients together in a large bowl except for the shortening and water, then add the shortening and mix just until the dough looks like coarse meal.

2. Stir in the water, 1 tablespoon at a time, until the dough just comes together. Turn the dough out onto a piece of plastic wrap and gather the ends together, forming the dough into a disk. Wrap with the plastic and chill for at least 30 minutes.

3. To roll out the pastry, follow steps 3 and 4 for Andy's Spice Crust (page 32).

MAKES A DOUBLE 9-INCH CRUST.

Short Crust Pastry

*T*his pastry is a sort of sweet pizza dough and can be used in many different ways. I use it for the Individual Berry Shortcake Pies page 230. I also like the idea of spreading good fruit curd or jelly on the crusts or piling them high with whipped cream and poached fruit.

³/₄ cup sifted all-purpose flour, chilled
Pinch of salt
6 tablespoons (³/₄ stick) unsalted butter, chilled and cut into 6 pieces
2 to 4 tablespoons iced water

1. Preheat the oven to 400°F.

2. In the bowl of a food processor fitted with the metal blade, combine the flour and salt. Add the butter and pulse several times until the flour looks a bit like cornmeal. With the motor running, pour the iced water down the feed tube, 1 tablespoon at a time, until the mixture just holds together.

3. Spread a piece of plastic wrap on the counter and turn the dough out of the processor bowl onto it. As you wrap the dough in the plastic, form it into a disk. Flatten the disk and refrigerate for 1 hour.

4. On a lightly floured surface, roll out the disk until it's approximately ⅛ inch thick. Using a saucer as a pattern, cut out 4 circles with a sharp knife. Place the dough circles on an ungreased baking sheet, prick them with a fork, and refrigerate for 30 minutes.

5. Bake the dough for 8 to 10 minutes or until the edges are light brown. Let cool completely.

MAKES 4 PASTRY CIRCLES.

Crumb Crusts

In counting the many virtues of crumb crusts, foremost in my mind comes the fact that they are quick and easy. They are anything but fair-weather friends—they're not temperamental and they won't embarrass you by falling apart. Delicate enough to complement a complex filling, they are also sturdy enough to withstand the juiciest fruit. To top it all off, you can make them out of just about any ingredients you have on hand—from crackers to cereal to the last stale cookies in the box.

These recipes are meant to be flexible guides. Use them as stepping-stones to creating your own distinct crusts by adding ingredients like nuts, coconut, or dried fruit or by adding a teaspoon of such flavorings as lemon, almond, or orange extract. And by no means limit your use of crumb crusts to the traditional recipes. I recommend using them with just about any dessert recipe, and I've also used a few—particularly the nut and cereal crusts—for main dish and hors d'oeuvre recipes with a vegetable filling.

Basic Graham Cracker Crust

1⅓ cups graham cracker crumbs (about 16 whole crackers)
¼ cup sugar
5 tablespoons unsalted butter, melted

1. Preheat the oven to 375°F.

2. In the bowl of a food processor fitted with the metal blade, process the graham crackers and sugar to fine crumbs.

3. With the motor running, add the butter and process until the crumbs are moist and stick together.

4. Press the graham cracker mixture into the bottom and sides of a 9-inch pie pan. Bake in the center of the oven for 8 minutes or until the edges are slightly brown.

MAKES A SINGLE 9-INCH CRUST.

Basic Cookie Crust

1½ cups cookies, such as vanilla wafers, Oreos, chocolate wafers,
zwiebacks, amaretto cookies, or gingersnaps
5 to 8 tablespoons unsalted butter, melted

1. Preheat the oven to 375°F.

2. In the bowl of a food processor fitted with the metal blade, process the cookies to fine crumbs. With the motor running, add 5 tablespoons of the melted

butter through the feed tube and process until the crumbs are moist and stick together, adding more butter if necessary for moistness.

3. Press the cookie mixture into the bottom and sides of a 9-inch pie pan. Bake in the center of the oven for 8 minutes or until the edges are slightly brown.

MAKES A SINGLE 9-INCH CRUST.

Granola Crust

1 cup granola cereal
$\frac{1}{2}$ cup chopped nuts, such as walnuts, peanuts,
or Brazil nuts
3 tablespoons sugar
5 to 8 tablespoons unsalted butter, melted

1. Preheat the oven to 375°F.

2. In the bowl of a food processor fitted with the metal blade, combine the granola, nuts, and sugar; pulse 3 or 4 times. You want a fairly fine-crumb texture. With the motor running, add 5 tablespoons of the melted butter through the feed tube and process until the crumbs come together, adding more butter if necessary.

3. Press the mixture into the bottom and sides of a 9-inch pie pan. Bake in the center of the oven for 8 minutes or until the edges are slightly brown.

MAKES A SINGLE 9-INCH CRUST.

Additions for Crumb Crusts

Nuts: Reduce the amount of cookie crumbs to 1 cup and add ½ cup finely ground walnuts, pecans, almonds, or hazelnuts.

Chocolate: Add 2 squares melted unsweetened chocolate.

Coconut: Add ½ cup flaked coconut.

Zest: Add a teaspoon of lemon or orange zest.

Spices: Add a teaspoon of ground cinnamon, allspice, or nutmeg.

Maple Syrup: Add up to a tablespoon to graham cracker, granola, and nut crusts.

Nut Crust

1 cup finely ground pecans, walnuts, or peanuts
2½ tablespoons sugar
5 to 8 tablespoons unsalted butter, melted

1. Preheat the oven to 375°F.

2. Blend the nuts and sugar together in a bowl. Add just enough melted butter to bind, then press the mixture into the bottom and sides of a 9-inch pie pan.

3. Bake in the center of the oven for 8 minutes or until the edges are slightly brown.

MAKES A SINGLE 9-INCH CRUST.

Corn Flake or Rice Cereal Crust

3 cups corn flakes or puffed rice cereal
1 tablespoon sugar
Approximately 4 tablespoons unsalted butter, melted

1. Preheat the oven to 375°F.

2. In the bowl of a food processor fitted with the metal blade, process the cereal to make 1½ cups crumbs.

3. Add the sugar, then pour in enough butter for the crumbs to come together.

4. Press the mixture into the bottom and sides of a 9-inch pie pan. Bake in the center of the oven for 8 minutes or until the edges are slightly brown.

MAKES A SINGLE 9-INCH CRUST.

Tart Crusts

A tart crust is a bit less delicate than a traditional crust. It is slightly stiffer in consistency and thus can withstand a little more handling. The first recipe is for a dessert crust. The second one is for a savory crust, perfect for hors d'oeuvres and supper dishes. In both cases, make sure you fold the pastry over double around the rim so that the edges won't crumble when you remove the tart form.

Dessert Tart Crust

1 cup plus 2 tablespoons sifted all-purpose flour, chilled
1½ teaspoons sugar
8 tablespoons (1 stick) unsalted butter, chilled and cut into 8 pieces
¼ cup iced water

1. In the bowl of a food processor fitted with the metal blade, pulse together the flour and sugar. Sprinkle the pieces of butter over the dry ingredients and pulse 3 or 4 times until the flour resembles cornmeal. Pour 1 tablespoon iced water down the feed tube and pulse once. Add another tablespoon and pulse. Continue adding tablespoons of iced water until the dough just holds together. Turn the dough out onto a sheet of plastic wrap. As you wrap the pastry in the plastic, form it into a flat disk. Refrigerate for 30 minutes.

2. Roll the dough out on a lightly floured surface until it's slightly larger than the tart pan. Drape one end of the dough over the pin, gently lift it, then slip the pan underneath the dough and lower it into the pan. Press the dough gently —and quickly—against the sides of the pan. Crimp edges as desired. Refrigerate the crust for at least 30 minutes before either filling or prebaking.

3. To prebake the tart crust, line the tart crust with foil and fill with dry beans or pastry weights (small nuts and bolts work well also). For a partially baked crust, place in the center of a preheated 350°F oven for 15 minutes. For a fully baked crust, remove the foil and the weights and continue baking for 3 to 5 minutes, until the crust is slightly brown.

MAKES A SINGLE 11-INCH CRUST.

Savory Tart Crust

This crust is even sturdier than the Dessert Tart Crust (page 40), making it perfect for elegant little hors d'oeuvres that you don't want to fall apart in your guests' laps. You can also use this recipe for one big supper tart.

1½ cups sifted all-purpose flour, chilled
12 tablespoons (1½ sticks) unsalted butter, chilled and cut into 12 pieces
Pinch of salt
2 to 3 tablespoons iced water

1. In a food processor fitted with the metal blade, process the flour, butter, and salt for 15 seconds, until the mixture resembles coarse cornmeal. With the motor running, pour 2 tablespoons of the water through the feed tube and process until the dough just holds together. Add more water by the teaspoon, if necessary. Turn the dough out onto a piece of plastic wrap. As you wrap the pastry in the plastic, form it into a flat disk. Refrigerate for 30 minutes.

2. If you're using the dough for an 11-inch tart pan, roll out the dough as directed on page 40 for the Dessert Tart Crust (step 2). Follow instructions at step 3 for prebaking instructions. For hors d'oeuvre tarts, butter miniature or standard-size muffin cups or lightly coat them with nonstick cooking spray. On a lightly floured surface, roll the dough into a thin circle. Cut out as many circles as you have muffin cups and press the circles into the cups. If you are using standard-size muffin cups, bring the dough only halfway up the sides of the cups. Prick the bottom of the shells and refrigerate them for 20 minutes before either filling or prebaking.

3. To prebake the tartlet shells, line each one with foil and fill with dry beans or pastry weights. For partially baked shells, place in the center of a preheated

350°F oven for 15 minutes. For fully baked shells, remove the foil and weights and continue baking for 3 to 5 minutes, until the shells are slightly brown.

4. Let cool on a wire rack. At this point the shells can be stacked in a plastic bag and frozen. Defrost to room temperature before filling.

MAKES A SINGLE 11-INCH TART CRUST, 24 STANDARD-SIZE TARTLET SHELLS, OR 36 MINI TARTLET SHELLS.

Pâte Brisée

*T*he best recipe I have found for supper pies. The pastry is sturdy yet tender, well worth the extra time and planning you have to put into making it. I talk more about this pastry in "What's for Dinner?" (page 157).

8 tablespoons (1 stick) unsalted butter,
chilled and cut into 8 pieces
3 tablespoons lard, chilled
2 cups sifted all-purpose flour, chilled
¼ teaspoon salt
6 to 7 tablespoons iced water

1. In a large mixing bowl, work the butter and lard into the flour and salt until only small lumps are apparent. Make a well in the center of the mixture and gradually pour in the iced water, 1 tablespoon at a time, mixing quickly with the edge of your hand slightly cupped and scooping from the outer edge into the middle, until you can just gather the dough into a ball. Add another tablespoon or 2 of water if the dough is still dry.

2. Turn the dough out onto a piece of plastic wrap. As you wrap the dough in the plastic, form it into a disk. Let the dough rest in the refrigerator for at least 2 hours or up to 2 days.

MAKES A SINGLE 9-INCH CRUST.

Pizza and Calzone Crust

*M*akes a very bready crust.

1 package active dry yeast
1 teaspoon sugar
½ cup warm water
1¼ cups sifted all-purpose flour
½ teaspoon salt
1½ teaspoons olive oil

1. In a small bowl, stir together the yeast and sugar, then add the water. Let stand for 10 minutes.

2. In the bowl of a food processor fitted with the metal blade, mix together the flour and salt. With the motor running, pour the yeast through the feed tube and process until the dough pulls away from the sides of the bowl. Add the oil through the feed tube and pulse 3 or 4 times.

3. Use the dough right away or, for a really tender crust, seal it in a lightly floured plastic bag and let it rest in the refrigerator for an hour.

MAKES ENOUGH DOUGH FOR A 12½-INCH THIN-CRUST PIZZA,
A 9-INCH THICK-CRUST PIZZA, OR A 10-INCH CALZONE.

Pâte à Choux

*P*âte à choux is a host's secret weapon. The dough can be put together in less than five minutes and, when baked, it puffs up into little golden nuggets. The dough can be flavored or the finished puffs can be stuffed with a variety of fillings (see "The Pleasure of Your Company," page 113, for filling suggestions).

³/₄ cup water
3 tablespoons unsalted butter
¹/₂ teaspoon salt
³/₄ cup sifted all-purpose flour
3 large eggs

1. Preheat the oven to 450°F.

2. In a large saucepan, bring the water to a boil, then add the butter and salt. When the butter is melted, reduce the heat to low and pour in the flour all at once. Stir hard with a wooden spoon until the flour is absorbed and the mixture becomes a thick dough. Remove the pan from the heat.

3. Transfer the dough to the bowl of a food processor fitted with the metal blade. With the motor running, add 1 egg at a time through the feed tube, processing until the dough is smooth and shiny.

4. Use the dough immediately or store it in an airtight container in the refrigerator for up to 2 days.

5. When you're ready to bake, drop teaspoon-size mounds of the dough about an inch apart onto a lightly oiled baking sheet. An alternative—and fancier—method is to use a pastry bag. Fit the bag with a medium tip, fill three-quarters of the way to the top with dough, and pipe the dough onto the prepared baking sheet.

6. Bake in the center of the oven for 8 minutes. Reduce the heat to 400°F and bake until the dough is browned, another 6 to 8 minutes. Let the puffs cool on the baking sheet, then remove to a wire rack.

7. The puffs will keep for several months in an airtight container in the freezer. To reheat, place the frozen puffs on a baking sheet in a 375°F oven for about 8 minutes.

MAKES ENOUGH FOR ABOUT 80 SMALL HORS D'OEUVRES.

Biscuit Crust

This is one of the easiest—and quickest—crusts for a supper pie. Since it cannot endure a liquid filling — it becomes very soggy and falls apart — it should be used only for a top crust and, even then, it shouldn't be put on until the last stages of cooking.

2 cups sifted all-purpose flour, chilled
3 teaspoons baking powder
1 teaspoon salt
6 tablespoons vegetable shortening, chilled and cut into 6 pieces
$^2/_3$ to $^3/_4$ cup cold milk

1. Sift the dry ingredients together into a large bowl. Cut in the shortening until the mixture resembles cornmeal.

2. Make a well in the center of the flour and pour in $^1/_2$ cup milk. Mix very lightly with a fork. If necessary, add enough additional milk to incorporate any dry flour and make the dough moist enough to form into a ball. Turn out the dough onto a lightly floured surface and knead gently a few times. Then lightly roll it flat, starting at the center and rolling away from you until it's about $^1/_4$ inch thick.

3. Use this dough all in one piece, laying it gently over the top of a hot filling, or cut out shapes from the dough and layer the shapes over the filling. Dab the edges where the shapes touch with a little cold water, then gently press to seal the shapes together. Bake as directed in the recipe you are using.

MAKES A SINGLE 9-INCH CRUST OR ABOUT 8 BISCUITS.

Biscuit Crust Additions

You can vary the basic biscuit crust recipe by adding ingredients that complement your filling. Here are some suggestions:

Grated cheese

Finely chopped and lightly sautéed onions

Finely chopped jalapeño pepper

Finely chopped garlic

Chopped fresh herbs, such as chives, thyme, rosemary, oregano, or basil

Paprika, ground red pepper, cumin, coriander, chili powder, or other dried spices

Individual Mashed Potato Crusts

*T*his was a secret recipe of my mom's that came to represent Tuesday night dinners for me. Sunday we always ate a big roast beef supper with roasted potatoes. Monday we had leftover beef in gravy with noodles. Tuesday my mom mashed the leftover roasted potatoes and made them into individual crusts, then filled them with whatever was left of the beef—usually shredded and bound with a sauce she made using Campbell's cream of mushroom soup. Sometimes my dad would drag someone who needed a good hot meal home from work, and when they saw these little crusts brimming with a kind of creamed chipped beef, they fell in love with my mom.

About 3 cups leftover mashed potatoes
Melted butter, for drizzling

1. To make the crusts, line a small, shallow casserole dish (about 4 inches long and 2 inches wide) with aluminum foil, leaving a good amount hanging over the sides for easy removal. Spray the foil lightly with a nonstick cooking spray.

2. Spoon some of the mashed potatoes into the casserole dish, pressing them up the sides and making sure you have a good thick layer on the bottom.

3. Remove the mashed potatoes from the casserole with the foil holding them in shape and place on a baking sheet. Repeat steps 1 and 2 until all of the mashed potatoes are used up.

4. Place the baking sheet in the freezer just until the potatoes are firm, then wrap them well with the foil overhang. They'll keep for a month in the freezer.

5. To use the crusts, preheat the oven to 350°F. Partially unwrap the tops of the frozen crusts and place on a baking sheet. Drizzle a little melted butter into the center of each crust, then place a sheet of foil loosely over the top of all of them.

6. Bake for 30 minutes in the center of the oven. Take off the top layer of foil and bake for another 15 minutes or until the shells are brown.

7. To serve, spoon a hot filling into the center of each crust.

MAKES 6 INDIVIDUAL MASHED POTATO CRUSTS.

Phyllo Dough, Dumpling Skins, and Empanada Wrappers

Phyllo Dough

Phyllo dough makes a wonderful crust for pies. You can use several whole sheets for one crust or you can cut the phyllo into strips and make small packages or bundles for hors d'oeuvres. Phyllo dough, which is sold in the frozen-food section of most supermarkets or in stores specializing in Greek or Middle Eastern food, comes rolled up in a box, the sheets of dough separated by wax paper.

The trick to using phyllo is to keep it moist and to work quickly and without interruptions. Take the roll of sheets out of the box and carefully unroll. Cover the stack of flat sheets with a moist kitchen towel. Lay the first sheet of phyllo down in a greased pie pan or on a greased baking sheet. Brush melted butter over the surface, then add another sheet. Repeat at least 4 more times. Add filling, then begin to cover it with more phyllo sheets, each time coating the layer with butter before adding another sheet.

A pie made with a phyllo crust takes about 30 to 35 minutes to cook in a 375°F oven. Let rest for 5 to 10 minutes before serving.

Dumpling Skins and Empanada Wrappers

There are cookbooks that will lead you through how to make the pastry for both dumpling skins and empanada wrappers. This one won't. I used to do it when I was younger, had more time, and didn't live in a neighborhood where I could purchase both easily. If you're not so lucky, they're both easy to make and worth doing at least once in your lifetime—on a quiet day. For dumplings, I have used the recipe in *The Thousand Recipe Chinese Cookbook* by Gloria Bley Miller. Susan Purdy's *As Easy as Pie* is a good source for a workable empanada recipe.

Commercial dumpling skins and empanada wrappers both come stacked in plastic bags. They can be kept frozen, tightly sealed, for up to 6 months. When you are ready to use either of them, take the package out of the freezer and let sit for 15 minutes. Remove however many skins or wrappers you'll need, then carefully reseal the bag and return to the freezer. Cover the skins or wrappers you will use with a damp cloth while you make one of the fillings suggested in "The Pleasure of Your Company" (page 113), then follow the directions here to fill them.

To make dumplings: Place a little less than a teaspoon of filling in the middle of each skin. Moisten the edges with water and fold one edge over the filling to meet the opposite edge. The dumpling will look like a half-moon with a plump tummy. Press all around to seal edges.

To make empanadas: Place an empanada wrapper on a lightly floured surface. Brush the edges of the dough with a little beaten egg, then place about a teaspoon of filling in the center. Fold the dough over to form a semicircle and press the edges to seal either by pressing a fork along the edges or crimping the edges with your fingers.

Dessert for Breakfast

Work and pray, live on hay,
You'll get pie in the sky when you die.

—JOE HILL, FROM A LABOR SONG, "THE PREACHER
AND THE SLAVE"

Y ou could do worse than start the day with a slice of pie. That's what I tell my husband whenever he sees our oldest son hunkered over a pie plate, steadily working through the remains of the previous night's dessert. The first time Chris saw him do this, Sam was five years old. Chris sought me out, and in a tone of voice that communicated a great deal of skepticism about my mothering techniques, he asked me if I knew what our child was having for breakfast.

"I made him some oatmeal," I answered.

"That's not what he's eating now."

"What's he eating, then?"

"Pie."

"So?"

"It's pie."

"Yeah?"

"It's eight o'clock in the morning," he said, clearly believing I had lost my senses. Chris is the most patient and kind of men, but I could see that he was deeply disturbed. I patted his cheek and appealed to the historian in him.

"Don't worry, honey," I assured him. "In the old days, people used to eat pie every morning and they went on to lead productive lives."

Although Chris didn't buy it, what I told him is true. From the early colonial days until the late nineteenth century, pies were a staple in the kitchen pantry. Little thought was given to the nutritional contribution they made to the daily diet. Instead, pies were appreciated for the way they efficiently filled empty stomachs in the short time that was available before the workday began.

In fact, nutrition wasn't considered at all until the 1880s. Influenced by the growing popularity of science, a movement called the New England Kitchen was concocted by one Wilbur O. Atwater. He believed that America was being drained of its preeminent strength by the bad eating habits of the new immigrants and the working poor who inhabited the cities' slums. Their living standards could be changed, he preached, not by increasing wages or even improving their housing, but by managing what they ate. The diet he came up with in his experiments relied heavily on overcooked, cheap cuts of meats; he eschewed fresh fruits and vegetables (he considered canned and processed foods to be more nutritious); and he totally rejected such staples as flour, grains, and potatoes (unless the potatoes were first pared to remove all skin and then boiled to a soft mush). "Beset with false pride of show and the petty ambition to go ahead of their neighborhoods," he wrote, "they [the poor] continue to purchase the finest flour and expel their limited resources and energy on wasteful dishes."

The magazines of the time took up his cause. Sara Tyson Rorer, a noted cooking teacher and the food editor for *Ladies' Home Journal,* declared, "All forms of so-called pie are to be condemned." In discussions of the social upheaval of the time, pies were often mentioned as impediments to change. The German

Cowboys and Pies

As people lit out for the West, they sustained themselves with many a pie. Dried apples were an essential supply of the wagon train's mess, and a favorite breakfast was apple pie and something called bachelor pie, which was made from a quick biscuit dough and any handy filling. When supplies ran low, cooks on the wagon trains used their ingenuity. A cookbook entitled *Information for Everybody: An Invaluable Collection of About Eight Hundred Practical Recipes*, published in 1866 and mentioned in a few cowboy memoirs, recommended adding rendered drippings from the fat of a just-killed steer to flour if the lard was used up. Oliver Nelson, a cook who worked on the wagons traveling along the Chisholm Trail, recalled in his memoir, *The Cowman's Southwest*, serving pies filled with prairie oysters (bull testicles), sliced thin and fried in bacon grease, when the apple barrel was empty.

sociologist Werner Sombart saw the dream of American socialism dashed on "the reefs of roast beef and apple pie" that fed the nation. Prominent reformers such as Jane Addams and Jacob Riis espoused at least some of Atwater's principles and advocated setting up cooking classes in settlement houses and public schools in an attempt to steer immigrants away from cultivating the American taste for sweets and pastries. The American Public Health Association even saw a correlation between the vast consumption of heavy, hard-to-digest pastry (especially in such dishes as Irish meat pies and Italian tortes) and men in the slums drinking too much.

It's unclear how successful Mr. Atwater was in helping either the poor or the immigrants with his New England Kitchen movement. He did, however, find converts among the rising number of middle-class women who, tired of spending a lot of time in the kitchen and faced with a shortage of people willing to go into home service, embraced his simpler recipes. Very few pie recipes made it into Atwater's cooking repertory, and he saw no reason why breakfast should include anything but a piece of toast, some fruit, cereal "wafers," and a bit of stimulant, as he was fond of calling coffee and tea. Mr. Atwater, I am sure, did not look fondly upon the idea of eating a slice of pie in the morning. It would just be wrong: old-fashioned, sinful, dangerous, foolhardy. Wrong!

By the end of the First World War, farms were about the only places in the country where you could find pie on the breakfast table. Women's magazines and home economics teachers continued preaching the principles of the New England Kitchen movement, but pies were too essential a part of farm life to be abandoned.

I grew up in a city and except for the leftover pie my brother and I got up early every Monday to eat, I never actually saw anyone have pie for breakfast, that is until I first went away to college. I left for college the same summer I graduated high school as the only legitimate means I had of getting away from home. It was a state school, buried in the foothills of the Pennsylvania Appalachians. In the valley below the mountains, the farms spread out in blocks of green and tan, anchored by little bitty towns consisting only of a church and a gas station catty-corner to each other across a two-lane blacktop.

A Vermont farmwife's 1877 housekeeping records include a list of the 421 pies she made that year. In November 1865, Mrs. Nettie Spenser, keeping house in the wilderness of the new state of Minnesota, wrote in her diary that she baked 200 gooseberry pies over a few days' time and froze them in the snow outside her kitchen door in order to get her family through to the spring thaw.

One memory I have of that summer, besides being thrown out of school, was the math tutor who took me for a ride on his motorcycle up a steep mountain road. Once at the top, we proceeded to get so drunk that he couldn't drive the bike back down. Another memory from that summer that has stuck with me is of eating breakfast with my father every couple of Saturdays at a roadhouse just outside of town. He had taken a leave of absence from his work in the city to conduct a course in community organizing (Rabble-Rousing 102, he called it) at a state college a few miles away from the one I was attending. On the weekends that he went home to see my mom and brother, he'd stop in to check up on me. Most of the time I was hung over and resented being dragged from bed so early in the morning. As we'd enter the roadhouse and he'd greet everyone with what I thought of as excessive goodwill, I'd walk far behind him and scowl. That summer he wore madras walking shorts from which his long skinny legs shot out like roots. And on his head he wore a beat-up old baseball cap that he pulled low over his glasses. He'd call the waitress "darlin'" in an Irish brogue as she poured him his first cup of coffee, then order one egg sunny-side up, some hash browns, and bacon. I stuck with hash browns and a milk shake and when the waitress was gone, my dad would ask me how I was doing. I'd say fine; he'd say good, then spread out the local newspaper and begin reading. That's when I'd start looking around at what other people were doing and notice the slices of cherry and lemon meringue pie that were disappearing from behind the glass doors of the revolving dessert display.

After a couple of these outings, I brought this odd habit to my dad's attention. He looked around the room, at the other tables where the remains of pancakes and eggs were being pushed aside for a serving of rhubarb-apple pie, and he thought it was pretty weird, too.

"How come people eat pie so early around here?" he asked the waitress when she came around to refill his coffee cup. I covered my face behind a sheet of my hair, but listened for her answer.

"There's no bad time for pie," she said.

"Isn't it kind of early, though?"

"You're from the city, aren't you?" she asked, almost flirtatiously I thought.

"Philadelphia," Dad replied.

"Well, our days start a little earlier around here. It's almost afternoon by our clocks."

After she left, he laughed and shook out the paper. "Should be near midnight for you, then," he said to me. "Go on and have a slice."

So I did — peach à la mode — and it was just fine.

I was kicked out of that school by the end of the summer and found myself dumped back home. Although my brother and I were both nearly grown and hardly needed such looking after, my mom continued to make a pie every Sunday afternoon out of habit. I often started my day nibbling through the dwindling remains of one of those pies. Sometimes, when my friends and I went out for breakfast after a late-night party, I would order pie despite their remarks about how gross it was to dig into so much meringue at five in the morning. I'd tell them to be quiet, knowing it was the only thing of value I'd learned at college.

I've learned a few other lessons since then, but one of the most important is that a freshly baked pie, made expressly for breakfast, can't be beat, though it does take some advance planning. The thought of rolling out dough at dawn is enough to dampen even *my* hunger for pie in the morning, so I prepare a crust the night before, cover it in plastic wrap, and put it in the refrigerator. Depending on the kind of pie I'm planning, I might even prepare the filling, blending eggs and cream, or cutting fruit to store in the refrigerator as well. No matter how bleary I am in the morning, I can throw the ingredients together, put on the kettle for a cup of tea, and by the time I've achieved some semblance of consciousness, the pie is done and the people around me, even my puritan husband, have forks in hand, professing their undying love for me.

It goes without saying that you don't want a very rich pie for breakfast (unless, of course, it's left over from the night before and is beckoning to you from a refrigerator shelf). The best breakfast pies have a clean taste and are made with minimal cream and few seasonings that might startle a waking stomach. The more substantial of the pies featured in this chapter make terrific late-night suppers and are best served hot in the winter with beer or wine or at room temperature in the summer along with something very cold to drink. During the holidays I keep one or two extra pies in the freezer, to serve when the house fills up with overnight guests or when we come home late from a party and need a midnight snack. As our pioneer ancestors understood, it's really not that much more work to make an extra pie. And the benefits are boundless.

Marriage Pie

*T*his is called a marriage pie because it calls for two different fruits that complement each other yet hold on to their own flavors. Here, I call for blackberries and apricots, two fruits that not only taste lovely together but also look handsome lying next to one another. When matching up different fruits, be sure to choose one that is sweet and one that is tart.

Single 9-inch Butter and Lard Crust (page 25), baked

Filling:
1 cup sugar
4 tablespoons all-purpose flour
2 cups fresh blackberries, washed and hulled
1 tablespoon fresh lemon juice
1½ tablespoons confectioners' sugar
6 or 7 fresh apricots, peeled, pitted, and thinly sliced
Whipped cream, for serving

1. Prepare the crust.

2. In a large saucepan, combine the sugar and flour. Add all of the blackberries except for a small handful and mash together slightly. Bring the mixture to a boil over low heat, stirring constantly. Add the lemon juice.

3. Sprinkle the confectioners' sugar over the bottom of the pie crust. Arrange the apricots over the sugar and pour the blackberry mixture over the apricots. Chill for at least 2 hours. Just before serving, sprinkle the reserved berries over the top of the apricots. Serve with whipped cream.

S E R V E S 6.

Rustic Fruit Tart

My sister, Sue, makes this tart on Sundays in the summer. Sometimes she makes it to celebrate a special occasion, such as a birthday, but just as often she does it because it helps her to release the stress of a hard week at work and because the fruit in her garden is in bloom. She'll take the tart out to the table with a pitcher of iced tea and the Sunday paper and soon neighbors and my brother (who she swears can smell something good cooking from his house a mile away) are coming through her garden gate. Before long, the tart is gone, and she's feeling much better.

This tart is actually like a square pizza. The crust used in this recipe comes out a little harder than the usual tart crust, which makes it ideal for eating with your hands.

Crust:
2 cups sifted all-purpose flour, chilled
1 teaspoon sugar
8 tablespoons (1 stick) unsalted butter, chilled and cut into 8 pieces
1 large egg yolk
⅓ cup iced water

Filling:
3 cups mixed seasonal fruit, such as apples, pears, berries,
or semiripe melons, cut into small pieces
½ cup finely chopped nuts
½ cup sugar or more (to taste)
4 tablespoons (½ stick) unsalted butter,
cut into small pieces

1. Preheat the oven to 400°F.

2. In the bowl of a food processor fitted with the metal blade, pulse together the flour and sugar. Cut in the butter and quickly pulse 2 or 3 times, leaving large chunks of the butter in the mixture. Add the egg yolk and water through the feed tube and pulse just until the dough comes together.

3. Scrape the dough out of the bowl onto a lightly floured surface. Roll the dough out into a rough rectangle about 1¾ inches thick. Loosely wrap the dough around a rolling pin and unroll it onto a 12 × 16-inch ungreased baking sheet.

4. Sprinkle the fruit, nuts, and ½ cup sugar over the top of the dough. Fold the rim of the dough over the outermost fruit, making sure there's a deep enough rim to catch the fruit juice. Sprinkle the butter pieces over the top of the fruit and, if you wish, add a little more sugar.

5. Bake in the center of the oven for 1 hour or until the crust is golden. Cool on a wire rack and serve.

SERVES 8 OR MORE, DEPENDING ON THE SIZE
OF THE SQUARES YOU CUT.

Shaker Lemon Pie

*T*his is my brother's Sunday pie recipe, and he tells me that it is always his intention to serve it for dessert after dinner but that it never lasts that long. Joe is a let's-open-the-refrigerator-and-see-what-we-have kind of cook, meaning he rarely follows a recipe, which sometimes leads to very strange creations (like hot dog crêpes or, one time, black bean, ham, and cheddar cheese omelets), but generally he's a fine cook, indeed. He told me that he found this recipe somewhere, he just can't remember where. It's an old traditional pie, and when I tried it out, I could see why it never lasts until dinner.

Double 9-inch Betty's Pie Crust (page 24), unbaked

Filling:
2 large lemons with thin rinds
2 cups sugar
4 large eggs, well beaten

1. Prepare the pastry. Line a 9-inch pie pan with half of the pastry and set aside in the refrigerator, along with the unrolled half, while you make the filling.

2. Cut the lemons into quarters, discard the seeds, and place in a food processor fitted with the metal blade. Process the lemons until very finely chopped, transfer to a medium bowl, then mix with the sugar. Let sit for at least 2 hours at room temperature. (Overnight is even better as long as you stir the mixture occasionally so that the sugar doesn't settle to the bottom.)

3. Preheat the oven to 450°F.

4. Add the eggs to the lemon mixture and pour the filling into the prepared crust. Roll out the remaining dough and lay it over the filling. Crimp the pastry over the rim and slash a few vents near the center of the top crust to allow steam to escape.

5. Bake in the center of the oven for 15 minutes, then reduce the heat to 375°F and cook for another 20 minutes or until the crust is golden brown.

SERVES 6.

Breakfast Pasties

I know a proper pasty is made with lamb, but for breakfast I like this one that my mom came up with when she married my father.

Much to her dismay, my mother found herself hitched to a tall, rail-thin man who couldn't have cared less about meals. They had gone out together for nearly four years before they married, and she had always assumed that his lack of interest in food was because no one in his house cooked much. His mother had died when he was twenty, and his house was ruled by a gang of beautiful and very popular sisters who had better things to do with their time than feed the men in the family. My mom figured she'd fatten him up in no time, but in the forty-five years they lived together he never gained an ounce.

My grandmother used to make a huge batch of pasties every Saturday night for dinner and my mother's brothers always fought over who would eat the leftovers. In the first months of her married life, Mom simply followed her mother's lead and made her own large batch and, to her happy surprise, my dad liked them so much that he continued to snack on them throughout the night and again the next morning when they got home from church. It was, she claims, the first dish she ever saw my dad eat with relish and it gave her hope. But the idea of her husband eating steak on Sunday mornings was upsetting to her, so she began to make two different varieties—a traditional meat pasty and another one with fruit or applesauce or breakfast sausage or Scrapple inside. (If you have to ask what Scrapple is, I can't tell you. Suffice it to say that the next time you're in the Philadelphia/New Jersey region, stop at a supermarket and pick up a package—it's usually sold in the aisle with such equally unhealthy foods as bacon and hot dogs. Follow the cooking directions and *don't* read the list of ingredients.)

The crust for this recipe is what I think of as a "hard" crust. When baked, it is substantial enough to pick up whole and it won't crumble when you bite into it. This makes it ideal for picnic foods and snacks to pack and take with you, or for young children who won't sit still to eat.

In terms of fillings, use your imagination. Short of cereal, whatever you like for breakfast can be put in a pasty. However, if you want to make your pasties with anything other than fruit, omit the confectioners' sugar from the pastry ingredients. Possibilities include cut-up fruit, such as apples or pears, dusted with cinnamon and nutmeg; strawberries, plums, or peaches sprinkled with sugar to taste; browned sausages (fat well drained); cubed ham; and cubed cheese, such as Gruyère, goat, feta, or Brie.

Short Crust Pastry:
2¼ cups sifted all-purpose flour, chilled
¼ teaspoon salt
½ cup lard, chilled
⅓ cup unsalted butter, chilled
1 tablespoon confectioners' sugar (with fruit fillings only)
1 large egg yolk
3 tablespoons iced water
1 beaten egg mixed with a little milk, to brush pastry

Approximately 2 cups filling of your choice

1. To make the pastry, sift the flour and salt into a mixing bowl. Cut the lard and butter into small pieces and mix them into the flour until they are well coated. Using your fingertips, rub in the fat until the mixture resembles fine bread crumbs. Stir in the sugar. Combine the egg yolk with the water and pour into the flour mixture. Mix quickly until a dough forms. Knead lightly in the bowl, then wrap in plastic and chill in the refrigerator for 30 minutes.

2. Prepare the filling of your choice.

3. Preheat the oven to 400°F.

4. Roll out the pastry to approximately ¼ inch thick. Using a saucer or upturned bowl, cut it into circles about 6 inches in diameter. Place approximately 3 tablespoons filling in the middle of each round.

5. Brush the rim of each round with the egg-milk mixture and fold the sides up over the filling to meet in the middle. Pinch the edges together and shape each pasty into a gentle mound. Make 2 slits on either side of the crest from which steam can escape. Brush the tops with the egg-milk mixture.

6. Put the pasties on a greased baking sheet. Bake for 10 minutes in the center of the oven, then reduce the heat to 350°F and bake for 20 minutes more or until golden brown.

MAKES 4 OR MORE GOOD-SIZE PASTIES, DEPENDING
ON SIZE OF CIRCLES.

Jelly Pie

*T*his is another of my mother's recipes, one she used to make when my brother or sister or I was sick and needed an extra dose of care. It comes out like a big circle of warm jelly toast.

Single 9-inch Butter and Lard Crust (page 25),
partially baked

Filling:
3 tablespoons all-purpose flour
1 cup sugar
1 tablespoon unsalted butter, melted
½ cup jelly (any flavor or variety will do, but the better
the quality, the better the taste)
2 large eggs, beaten

1. Prepare the crust.

2. Preheat the oven to 350°F.

3. Sift together the flour and sugar. Add the butter.

4. Combine the jelly with 1 cup warm water, then add to the flour-sugar mixture. Add the eggs and mix until just blended.

5. Pour into the pie shell and bake in the center of the oven for 15 minutes or until the edges of the crust are golden and the middle is set.

SERVES 6.

Cheese, Leek, and Ham Pie

I usually make two of these pies at a time and freeze one so that I have something on hand for late suppers, unexpected guests, or days when I am simply too tired to cook.

Single 9-inch Betty's Pie Crust (page 24), unbaked

Filling:
1 tablespoon unsalted butter
1 large leek, washed well and thinly sliced
2 cups milk
1 cup light cream
4 large eggs
2½ cups grated Swiss cheese
1 teaspoon dry mustard
1 teaspoon salt
¼ teaspoon freshly ground black pepper
½ cup Westphalian ham, diced

1. Prepare the crust and set aside in the refrigerator while you make the filling.

2. Preheat the oven to 375°F.

3. Melt the butter in a skillet. Add the leeks and sauté over medium heat until just wilted. Remove from the heat.

4. In a medium bowl, combine the milk and cream. Beat in the eggs. Add the leeks, cheese, mustard, salt, and pepper and stir until thoroughly mixed.

5. Sprinkle the ham on the bottom of the pie crust and pour the liquid filling over the ham.

6. Place the pie pan on a baking sheet and bake in the center of the oven for 50 minutes or until a knife inserted in the center of the pie comes out clean.

SERVES 6.

Potato and Egg Pie

*A*crust of thinly sliced potatoes makes this an untraditional pie. But it is absolutely delicious and very quick to prepare.

About 4 Idaho baking potatoes, skinned and sliced into thin rounds

Filling:
6 slices bacon
⅓ cup chopped scallions
2 tablespoons unsalted butter, cut into small pieces
8 large eggs
⅓ cup heavy cream
Salt and freshly ground black pepper to taste
Ground red pepper to taste

1. Cook the bacon in a 10-inch iron skillet over medium heat until crisp. Remove to a paper towel to drain. Add the scallions and cook until limp. Remove with a slotted spoon to a small plate and set aside.

2. Drain all but a slight slick of bacon drippings from the pan. Spray the skillet with nonstick cooking spray (or, if you don't count calories or cholesterol, add a tablespoon

67

of butter). Arrange the potato slices on the bottom and along the sides of the skillet, overlapping the slices to form a complete layer. Sprinkle with salt and pepper, then add another layer of potatoes. Dab with small, pea-size bits of butter. Cover and cook over medium heat for 15 to 20 minutes, until the potatoes are golden.

3. While the potatoes are cooking, beat together the eggs, cream, salt, black pepper, and ground red pepper. When the potatoes are ready, pour the egg-cream mixture over them.

4. Cover the pan and cook over low heat for about 8 to 10 minutes. Remove the lid and turn the oven to broil. Place the skillet under the broiler until the top of the pie puffs up and is completely set.

5. Crumble the bacon and sprinkle over the pie along with the scallions. Cut in wedges to serve.

SERVES 6.

Sausage and Egg Pie

A high-class Egg McMuffin. The eggs are cooked whole, almost poached, over the sausage and under a pastry crust. This is especially good when served with Fried Green Tomatoes (recipe follows).

Double 9-inch Butter and Lard Crust
(page 25), unbaked

Filling:
1 pound breakfast sausage, crumbled
(if using links, remove casing)

6 large eggs
2 tablespoons chopped fresh parsley
1 tablespoon chopped fresh chives
¼ teaspoon salt
⅛ teaspoon freshly ground black pepper
½ cup ricotta cheese (a rich plain yogurt, such as Brown Cow Farm,
may be substituted)

1. Preheat the oven to 425°F.

2. Prepare the pastry. Line a 9-inch pie pan with half of the pastry and set aside in the refrigerator, along with the unrolled half, while you make the filling.

3. Brown the sausage and drain very well, pressing the grease from the meat and draining on a paper towel. Sprinkle the sausage on the bottom of the crust.

4. Carefully break each egg, keeping the yolk whole, over the sausage. Sprinkle with the parsley, chives, salt, and pepper. Carefully spoon the ricotta cheese over and around the eggs.

5. Roll out the top crust, cover the pie with it, flute the edges, and slash a few vents across the top of the crust to allow steam to escape.

6. Bake for 30 minutes or until light brown.

SERVES 6.

Fried Green Tomatoes

This recipe comes from my friend Connie, who grew up on a farm near Plains, Georgia. She loves spicy food and adds up to three teaspoons ground red pepper to the cornmeal that coats the tomatoes in this recipe. I like spicy food, too, but over the years I've toned down her version to just half a teaspoon. Lucy may be mad at me for the change, but I have found that I like this dish more when I don't have to worry so much about singeing my taste buds.

2 large eggs beaten with a little milk
About 1½ cups sifted all-purpose flour
¾ cup yellow cornmeal
¼ to ½ teaspoon ground red pepper
6 thinly sliced green tomatoes
Olive oil, for frying
Kosher salt to taste

1. Arrange on the counter one bowl filled with the beaten eggs, another bowl with the flour, and one more with the cornmeal mixed with the ground red pepper.

2. Dredge the tomato slices in the flour and shake off the excess. Dip each slice into the egg and then coat with the cornmeal, shaking off the excess lightly.

3. Heat the oil in a large skillet over medium heat. When hot, add the tomatoes. Cook several minutes, until golden, then turn and cook on the other side. Drain on a paper towel and sprinkle with salt.

SERVES 6.

Corn Pie

A couple of times while I was living in Atlanta, I was invited to Sunday breakfast at the home of Miss Lucy Baldwin, who lived in Decatur. Miss Baldwin had a large garden and most of what she cooked either grew or was nurtured there. This dish was always included in the huge spread she put out. Most of the dishes were already made by the time I arrived, having been prepared the night before so she and her family could attend church and come home to eat a great breakfast without much work. I always wanted to ask her if I could come over and watch her cook but I was shy and never did, which continues to be one of the things I truly regret from my youth. I did, however, get recipes the last time I was invited. For this pie, which has no crust, the corn needs to be very, very fresh. It goes especially well with scrambled eggs.

8 ears fresh corn (to yield about 4 cups kernels)
3 large eggs
1½ cups milk
1 tablespoon sugar
Salt and freshly ground black pepper to taste
1 teaspoon grated onion
½ cup heavy cream
3 tablespoons unsalted butter
Paprika to taste

1. Preheat the oven to 325°F.

2. Slice the corn from the cob into a well-buttered, deep, 10-inch glass or clay pie pan.

3. In a large bowl, beat the eggs until light and foamy. Add the milk, sugar, salt, and pepper and beat until well blended. Stir in the onion. Stir the egg mixture into the corn.

4. Pour the cream on top of the corn mixture, dot with the butter, and sprinkle with paprika.

5. Bake, uncovered, for 35 to 40 minutes, until a knife inserted into the middle comes out clean. Cut into wedges or squares and serve warm.

SERVES ABOUT 6 GENEROUSLY.

Sitting Around Gabbing in the Afternoon

Children aren't happy with nothing to ignore,
And that's what parents were created for.

—OGDEN NASH, "THE PARENT"

When my second son, Al, was born, I planned to stay at home. I envisioned peaceful mornings writing, and long, joyous afternoons of nursing, reading, and cuddling with Al and my first son, Sam, who was just turning five. The basis for this vision was my experience with Sam, who took two long naps a day until well into his third year and who was good-natured and easygoing when awake. Soon after Sam was born, however, our precarious finances dragged me back to work, leaving Chris, who was finishing his doctoral work, to take care of Sam through most of his infancy. What I remembered from that time, and longed for with the new baby, was the gratification Chris experienced in each step of Sam's growth and the proprietary pride he took in how well he diapered, fed, and schlepped our son through busy days of studying, writing, and playing. I wanted to put at rest the envy I could still taste for the deep, abiding bond between my husband and Sam, a bond that developed in a more natural way than my own did.

So when Al was on the way, I got my boss at the newsletter to agree to a long sabbatical, then gave birth to what more experienced parents might have anticipated and what my mother described two months later as "a handful."

"You're going to need help," she warned as she packed her bags after spending a few days with us. My sister told me later that my mom reported that she had never seen a baby put a house in such an uproar.

"You know how she exaggerates," my kind sister tried to console me. "I mean, you're not still letting him stay up all night, are you?"

I couldn't tell her that three weeks after I brought Al home from the hospital, I was ready to declare a full retreat. Al preferred (and still does, for that matter) the night. At four months, I finally got him to grudgingly accept a late bedtime but, in the bargain, he canceled naps during the day. It was as if he had too much to do and no time to waste. He first climbed out of his crib at five months and from the moment he hit the floor he was off, a whirl of dust bunnies floating behind him. By six months he was cruising the perimeters of the rooms on his feet and at seven months he walked upright down the stairs, on his own, without falling. His favorite toy was a six-foot ladder that he discovered one day when I was attempting to plaster some of the holes in our living room walls. (We had bought the house dirt cheap two years earlier because it lacked such amenities as ceilings, electricity, and a working kitchen. After the down payment and the purchase of a few appliances for a makeshift kitchen, we were broke, and the house challenged visitors' perceptions of "habitable" for many years.) Al would scale the ladder to one of the top steps and crow with pride as he surveyed the rubbled horizon of his domain.

I was addled with sleeplessness, weary with keeping him safe, and, at the same time, trying to keep Sam happy and amused on the days he wasn't in nursery school. Not only was I not writing, I wasn't even thinking except to real-ize I had made a terrible mistake. Some days were better than others, of course, but I could not pretend that I wasn't miserable. I understand now that my unhappiness had more to do with myself than with my baby; when I mentioned to his doctor that I thought he was, perhaps, a little too energetic, she narrowed her very sensible eyes at me and said, "There's nothing wrong with him. Al's just being a baby." She then suggested that Chris and I get away for a weekend we couldn't afford, let alone accomplish. With our roles reversed, Chris took over as much as he could at night and on weekends, but the days stretched endlessly before me and the only help I prayed for was to be delivered from this hell and to have this child, indeed both these children, taken far, far away from me.

And I truly wanted that: to be free, not to have the burden any longer of pretending I was a competent mother. How much I loved Al and how much I just wanted to be rid of him! It felt awful to admit this to myself, and for many weeks I couldn't even form the desire into words. Heavy with guilt, weepy with despair, the only remedy I could come up with was to find my way into our dis-mal kitchen and lose myself in the intricate workings of a recipe.

Most of the time I chose to make pies, not just because I liked them, but because I could make them fairly quickly. A pie doesn't take a whole lot of concentration or expensive ingredients and, done with flair, pie-making is an art form, one that gives me a sense of accomplishment, which, back then espe-cially, I sorely needed. Before Al walked, I strapped him in a backpack while I baked; later I drew up a chair and let him stand beside me while I tried for the perfect crust.

"What are all these pie shells in here?" my mom asked when, concerned about my mental health, she visited again.

"I'm practicing," I told her. I don't think the sight of empty pie shells crowding out everything else on the refrigerator shelves assured her that I was sane, but she at least admitted I seemed less agitated than before.

"Make a proper pie and invite some friends over," she said.

"Why?"

She sighed a weary smile. "How do you think I got through you?"

The question *had* occurred to me—how did my mom and all the other moms I knew growing up, all of whom stayed at home without babysitters or even much support from their husbands, do this? This mothering thing?

How they did it, my mother explained, was by banding together, all of the neighborhood mothers drawing into a protective circle facing away, if only for an hour, from their kids. The families in my childhood neighborhood were young and growing. Carriages and prams were parked outside all the back doors on fine days. Under the flapping diapers on the clotheslines, the tiny muddy yards were crowded with swing sets, sandboxes, and toys. Once or twice a week, after the older children were safely back from school and before dinner needed to be started, most of the mothers on the block came to our house. In warm weather, the mothers would sit in our backyard under the apple tree or they would gather on the front steps; in winter, they would crowd into the narrow kitchen around the long table my dad made from an old door.

Unless there was a lot of blood or no movement, the mothers did not want to see or hear from their children. There was something about the way that group of women sat huddled close together, something in the low intensity of their voices, that warned us away. Even young babies were placed in playpens and strollers, away from laps and arms. I can't remember what my mother gave the women to drink, but I know there was always something sweet to eat, the remnants of the previous night's dessert, which, despite my dad's complete apathy about food, my mother continued to make. Cookies, cherry pies, 1-2-3-4 cakes, and puddings were always available at our house. To be sure, the women in our neighborhood did diet. (I remember Mrs. Coogan, the neighborhood bohemian, running down the block one day in her wedding dress, the long satin train snapping out behind her like a whip as she careened into our house yelling, "Look, I got into it again!") But I believe the sweets my mother served to these women were devoured with a special voracity born from a need for both comfort and friendship as they soldiered through the young years of motherhood.

I thought over my mom's suggestion. But things were different now, or at least I thought they were. Few parents remained at home, and the ones who did—those a friend of mine called "park" moms (the ones who hung out at the playground for hours with neat bags of nutritious snacks, the ones who knew every theory and principle of successful child rearing)—were not eager to come to a dilapidated house inhabited by a rambunctious savage and a very unpark-like, questionably sane mom. The only person I could entice at first was Fran, the mother of Sam's best friend. She was about to have her third child and was working part-time. On the day I called her for the first time with an offer of cherry pie and tea, her middle son had just washed her car keys down the drain-pipe in the backyard.

"I'll be right over," she said, and appeared five minutes later, carrying the defendant sideways across her swollen belly while her older son ran past her to find Sam. When Fran looked out the window to see where the children were going, what she saw was Al stark naked, balancing on the top rung of an old plastic jungle gym, pretending to be Indiana Jones (his whip a strip of insulation he'd pulled from the doorjamb).

"You see what he's doing?" she asked.

"You want sugar or honey?" I replied, gently coaxing her to the table.

I don't remember what we talked about but I know we laughed a lot. By the time she left and I started supper, I felt a little lighter and much more at ease.

It was surprising how quickly I found other desperate parents. For a while, I'd ask anyone I came across to come over. I used the pies as an excuse. I was testing pie recipes, I would say, and because they knew I wrote about food they came thinking they were going to get a real treat. But the quality of what

I served was of little importance to me. In fact, I remember a few lulus, but it hardly mattered. I needed distraction, Al needed socialization, and together we needed to break away into our own separate lives. Gradually I became more selective about who I invited to what Chris called my salon afternoons, and the friends I had over the most I grew to love with the kind of intensity that desperate situations create. We were war buddies. Over rhubarb pie and sometimes a fat glass of wine, we survived.

My mother, too, has remained friends with the women she came to know while she was trying to survive my infancy. I saw many of them at a party my mother gave recently. I sat among them and listened to the cadence of their voices, the same intimate whispers they used back in my mother's old kitchen. After their children were all finally in school, most of these women went back to work or finished college and took on new challenges outside of their homes and our neighborhood. Yet what they talked about that day was not their own accomplishments but those of their children; they swapped stories about wayward grandchildren and gave advice about how to handle retired husbands. They sounded a lot like my own friends, and I caught myself realizing how things *don't* change.

THE REASON A pie is perfect for company is that it can take as few as thirty minutes to actually prepare—less if you have dough in the freezer. At the risk of being summoned before the Culinary Inquisitor, I'll also admit that I'm not averse to using store-bought crusts, especially for occasions when serving pie is more about companionship than anything else. Crust mixes, frozen crusts, and the kinds of crusts that fold out of cellophane make pretty good shells, though even the best of them are fairly tasteless. For this reason, if you have to use a ready-made crust, it's probably best to stick to a single-crust recipe.

The best tool for making a quick pie is advance planning. Double a crust recipe whenever you make any pie, flatten the extra dough into a disk (which will defrost faster and more evenly than a ball will), wrap it well with plastic wrap, and throw it in the freezer, where it will keep just fine for the next six months. (I know some people who are organized enough to actually date their frozen dough. That's all very well and good, but I usually fall back on another method—the packet farthest back is the oldest; the amount of frost, like the rings of a tree, tells how old it is. Any package that I have to peel off of the ice cube trays, I automatically throw away.)

If you have a microwave, you can defrost dough very quickly. Just be careful it doesn't defrost all the way or the fat will melt. It's softened enough if the middle gives a little when you poke it with a finger. The time varies with microwave models but generally it takes around a minute and a half on high to defrost a small disk of dough.

Another time-saver is a crumb crust. There are all kinds, from the traditional graham cracker to nut, chocolate chip, coconut, or meringue. All of them are very easy to prepare and take less then five minutes if you have a food processor. The only thing to remember about these kinds of crusts is that they contribute an additional flavor to the overall taste of a pie. Although this would seem self-evident, it's often overlooked. You wouldn't, for instance, match a marshmallow-coconut crust with a lemon meringue filling.

The other point to remember about a quick pie is that it doesn't have to be beautiful. Believing that it must be is, I think, one of the hardest obstacles for modern cooks to overcome. It's a notion propagandized by food magazines and newspapers that show dishes meant for family meals looking as if they just came out of the kitchen of a five-star restaurant. I believe an unassuming pie is much more appropriate for sitting around with friends because it doesn't give off a pretentiousness that might take away from the real business at hand. The pie just needs to taste good. All anyone has to do is slip a slice on a plate, carry it into the living room, and eat it while curled up on the couch with a good friend. The flavors will loosen tongues, warm the senses, and restore the soul.

Al's Doodles

Here's a great way to bridge the 30 to 45 minutes between the time a pie goes into the oven and the time it comes out. It will also keep your guests from wandering around your house wondering why they came. My son thought up this quick recipe when he used to climb up on the counter and insist on helping me bake. I gave him the leftover dough scraps and a rolling pin I'd bought for him in a thrift store and he made what we came to call "doodles." They will hold over any hungry adult and delight children for being just their size.

Form the scraps of dough left over from crust-making into a ball and roll out into a ⅛-inch-thick sheet. Cut circles out of the dough with a biscuit cutter or the top of a juice glass and place on a baking sheet. Fill each circle with any jam or preserves you have on hand. Gather up the edges and pinch them together to seal. They should look like round little hats with a pom-pom of dough on top. Bake alongside the pie for about 10 to 15 minutes or until golden. Let cool for at least 5 minutes (the jam will be very hot inside, especially for kids) and serve slightly warm.

Cherry Pie

*T*his is my mother's recipe. A true cook of the fifties, she swears by canned products and makes this pie with canned cherry pie filling. I, however, make it with fresh cherries. The recipe calls for a double crust, but it can also be made with a bottom crust only.

Double 9-inch Butter and Lard Crust (page 25), unbaked

Filling:
$1\frac{1}{3}$ cups sugar
$\frac{1}{3}$ cup all-purpose flour
Pinch of salt
2 teaspoons kirsch (or a little more if it's been a bad day)
4 cups fresh, pitted sour cherries
2 tablespoons unsalted butter

1. Preheat the oven to 425°F.

2. Prepare the pastry. Line a 9-inch pie pan with half of the pastry and set aside in the refrigerator, along with the unrolled half, while you make the filling.

3. Combine the sugar, flour, and salt. Add the kirsch to the cherries and toss with the sugar-flour mixture to mix thoroughly. Turn into the prepared crust and dot with butter.

4. Roll out the remaining dough and lay it over the cherries. Press the edges together to seal and slash a few vents across the top of the crust to allow steam to escape.

5. Bake for 40 minutes or until the crust is golden.

SERVES 6.

Red Grape Pie

Although grapes are available all winter, I generally find myself baking this pie in the depths of February as a sort of feel-good treat to lift my mood.

Single 9-inch All-Butter Crust (page 26), unbaked

Filling:
5 cups seedless red grapes
²⁄₃ cup sugar
2¹⁄₂ to 3 tablespoons quick-cooking tapioca
1 teaspoon freshly grated lemon zest
1 teaspoon fresh lemon juice
2 tablespoons unsalted butter
Cinnamon sugar to taste
Ice cream, for serving

1. Preheat the oven to 425°F.

2. Prepare the crust and set aside in the refrigerator while you make the filling.

3. Combine the grapes, sugar, tapioca, lemon zest, and lemon juice in a large bowl. Pour into the pastry-lined pie pan. Dot with the butter and sprinkle with cinnamon sugar.

4. Place the pie pan on a baking sheet (the filling often spills over) and bake in the center of the oven for 35 to 40 minutes, until the rim of the pie is golden. Serve warm with ice cream.

S E R V E S   6.

Pear Pie

I love pears but the rest of my family doesn't. When I go to the market, I get carried away whenever I see an arrangement of them—I love their shape, their colors, the smell of them when they're almost ripe—and I end up buying more than I'll ever eat by myself. To get my family to help me eat the leftover pears, I'll poach them or make this pie, which they devour as long as I don't say anything about the pears inside.

*Single 9-inch All-Butter Crust (page 26) or
Butter and Lard Crust (page 25) or Basic Cookie Crust
(page 36) made with vanilla wafers and 2 tablespoons finely
crushed walnuts, unbaked*

Filling:
5 large Anjou pears
2 tablespoons frozen orange juice concentrate
½ teaspoon freshly grated lemon zest
¾ cup all-purpose flour
½ cup sugar
1 teaspoon ground cinnamon
½ teaspoon fresh ginger, peeled and grated
Pinch of salt
⅓ cup unsalted butter, at room temperature and cut into small pieces

1. Preheat the oven to 400°F.

2. Prepare the crust of your choice and place in the refrigerator while you make the filling.

3. Peel, core, and thinly slice the pears into a medium bowl. Add the orange juice concentrate and lemon zest and toss lightly. Arrange the slices in the pie shell (if you have time, in a pretty spiral; if you don't, in a pile). In a medium bowl, combine the flour, sugar, cinnamon, ginger, and salt. With the tips of your fingers, work in the butter until the mixture is crumbly. Sprinkle evenly over the top of the pears.

4. Bake in the center of the oven for 40 minutes or until the pears are tender and the edges of the crust are brown.

SERVES 6.

Bittersweet Lemon Tart

I found the recipe for this beautiful, rather elegant tart in a magazine called *The Pleasures of Cooking,* which used to be published by Cuisinart. This pie, which has an intense lemon flavor, has been known to chase away even the most stubborn winter blahs.

Single 11-inch Dessert Tart Crust (page 40), unbaked

Filling:
2 medium lemons, ends cut off
⅓ cup white rum
⅔ cup sugar
3 large eggs
8 tablespoons (1 stick) unsalted butter, at room temperature
and cut into 8 pieces

1. Preheat the oven to 350°F.

2. Prepare the crust and set aside in the refrigerator while you make the filling.

3. In the bowl of a food processor fitted with the slicing disk, process the lemons until finely cut. Transfer to a medium bowl and throw out all the seeds you can find.

4. Pour the rum over the lemons, cover tightly with plastic wrap, and let sit for at least 30 minutes or overnight. The longer the lemon mixture sits, the more heady (and potent) the flavor.

5. Fit the processor with the metal blade and process the soaked lemons until finely chopped. Add the sugar, eggs, and butter and process until the butter is completely incorporated. The mixture will look awful, as if curdled.

6. Place the prepared tart pan on a baking sheet and pour in the filling.

7. Bake for 30 minutes in the center of the oven. Increase the oven temperature to 400°F and bake for 10 minutes more or until the crust is golden.

SERVES 8 TO 10.

Rhubarb Pie

*J*oanie used to live up the block from our house, and she grew rhubarb in her backyard. Every time I visited her, she had a fresh rhubarb something to give me—from this pie to marmalade, cookies, and, once, a hair rinse made by steeping rhubarb in hot water. It was supposed to be good for redheads.

Try to use fresh rhubarb. You don't have to peel it, but you must separate the stalks and cut away the leaves, which are poisonous, then wash off any excess dirt and trim the bottoms.

Double 9-inch Betty's Pie Crust (page 24), unbaked

Filling:
4 cups fresh rhubarb, cut into ¹/₂-inch chunks
1¹/₄ cups sugar, plus extra for sprinkling over top crust
6 tablespoons all-purpose flour
2 teaspoons freshly grated lemon zest
¹/₄ teaspoon salt
¹/₃ cup honey
2 tablespoons unsalted butter

1. Preheat the oven to 400°F.

2. Prepare the pastry. Line a 9-inch pie pan with half of the pastry and set aside in the refrigerator, along with the unrolled half, while you make the filling.

3. Combine the rhubarb, sugar, flour, lemon zest, and salt in a large bowl and mix until the fruit is evenly coated. Blend in the honey and let stand for 5 to 10 minutes.

4. Spoon the rhubarb into the pastry-lined pie pan. Dot with the butter. Roll out the remaining dough. If you have time, make a lattice top crust; if you're pressed, try cutting out shapes and layering them across the top in a pretty pattern (see page 20 for instructions).

5. Sprinkle the top crust with sugar and bake in the center of the oven for 50 to 60 minutes, until the rim of the pie is golden.

S E R V E S   6.

Berry-Cheese Pie

I make this pie when my friend Joan's husband needs a quick fix for his cheesecake addiction. Joan has done me many favors, and her husband solves my computer problems when they crop up, so this pie is the least I can do in return. Instead of a traditional graham cracker crust, I often use a chocolate crumb or granola crust.

Single 9-inch Basic Graham Cracker Crust (page 36), baked

Filling:
8 ounces cream cheese, at room temperature
¼ cup sugar
1 teaspoon almond extract
2 large eggs

Berry topping:
2 cups fresh berries (such as raspberries, blueberries, or blackberries),
picked over and washed
⅓ cup water
1½ tablespoons cornstarch mixed in 2 tablespoons water

1. Prepare the crust.

2. Preheat the oven to 350°F.

3. In the bowl of a food processor fitted with the metal blade, process the cream cheese until smooth. Add the sugar, almond extract, and eggs and process until blended, scraping down the bowl if needed.

4. Pour the filling into the prepared crust and bake until just set, about 25 to 30 minutes. Let cool while you make the berry topping.

5. To make the topping, combine the berries and water in a saucepan and bring to a gentle boil. Reduce the heat and simmer for 5 minutes, stirring occasionally.

6. Remove from the heat and add the cornstarch mixture. Put back on the stove and bring to a boil for 1 more minute.

7. Cool to just warm and spoon over the pie.

SERVES 4 TO 6.

Lemon Pie

*M*y mother-in-law, Sally, gave me this recipe for one of the very few pies she had ever made. Sally was never a dessert eater but she believed that a dinner party should end with something sweet and she liked having people over for dinner. If she didn't make this pie, she made a pan of mint Jell-O with vanilla ice cream mixed in. I find both surprisingly satisfying.

Single 9-inch Basic Graham Cracker Crust (page 36), baked

Filling:
1⅓ cups sweetened condensed milk
⅔ cup fresh lemon juice
1¼ teaspoons freshly grated lemon zest
3 large egg yolks, slightly beaten

Meringue:
3 large egg whites
4 to 6 tablespoons sugar

1. Prepare the crust.

2. Mix together the condensed milk, lemon juice, lemon zest, and eggs in a medium bowl and pour into the crust. Set aside while you make the meringue.

3. Preheat the oven to 350°F

4. To make the meringue, beat the egg whites with an electric mixer until frothy, then begin to add the sugar, 1 tablespoon at a time, until stiff peaks form.

5. Pile the meringue on top of the filling, sealing the meringue to the edges of the crust.

6. Bake in the center of the oven for 10 to 15 minutes or until the meringue is golden.

SERVES 6.

Funeral Pie

*T*his nineteenth-century pie was actually served at weddings and other gatherings as well, but it was particularly popular for funerals because it's very quick to make. The version below was given to me by Mrs. Javie, a friend of my mother who told me her grandmother taught her how to make it. Mrs. Javie used to make it for her Saturday-night bridge parties.

Double 9-inch All-Butter Crust (page 26), unbaked

Filling:
1½ cups sugar
¼ cup all-purpose flour
Pinch of salt

2 cups water
1 cup raisins
1 large egg, beaten
2 tablespoons freshly grated lemon zest
3 tablespoons fresh lemon juice

1. Preheat the oven to 450°F.

2. Prepare the pastry. Line a 9-inch pie pan with half of the pastry and set aside in the refrigerator, along with the unrolled half, while you make the filling.

3. In the top of a double boiler, mix together the sugar, flour, and salt. Gradually add the water, stirring constantly. Stir in the raisins. Bring the mixture to a boil over *direct heat,* then cook for 1 minute, stirring constantly. Remove from the heat.

4. In a small bowl, combine the beaten egg with a little of the hot mixture, then stir the egg into the rest of the mixture in the top of the double boiler. Bring water to a simmer in the bottom of the double boiler, place the top of the double boiler over the simmering water, and cook for about 5 minutes, stirring constantly. Remove from the heat and add the lemon zest and juice. Cool slightly. (To cool fast, pop the mixture in the freezer for about 10 minutes.)

5. Pour the lemon mixture into the pie pan. Roll out the remaining dough and cut into ½-inch-wide strips. Lay the strips gently over the top of the filling. (You can make a lattice if you have the time, but this pie is also pretty with just single strips.)

6. Bake in the center of the oven for 10 minutes. Reduce the heat to 350°F and bake 20 minutes longer or until the top crust is golden brown.

S E R V E S 6 T O 8.

Molasses Pie

*B*ecause this pie is quick to make and comes out like a big fancy cookie, I often bake it for the Christmas fair at my sons' school. If you don't have a lemon on hand, try using an orange or even a grapefruit.

Single 9-inch Nut Crust (page 38), unbaked

Filling:
1 cup molasses
1 tablespoon all-purpose flour
1 lemon, cut into quarters

1. Preheat the oven to 425°F.

2. Prepare the crust and set aside in the refrigerator while you make the filling.

3. Blend the molasses and flour together in the bowl of a food processor. Add the lemon and process until finely chopped.

4. Pour the mixture into the prepared pie pan and bake for 10 minutes. Reduce the heat to 325°F and bake another 20 minutes or until a knife inserted in the center comes out clean.

S E R V E S 6.

Oatmeal Pie

*T*hink of this pie as a big oatmeal cookie. It takes an hour to bake but it is extremely easy to whip together. Serve and eat it as soon as it comes out of the oven, while it's still warm and gooey. It's very satisfying on a winter's afternoon when a heavy snow is lashing against the windowpanes.

Single 9-inch All-Butter Crust (page 26), unbaked

Filling:
4 tablespoons (¹/₂ stick) unsalted butter, at room temperature
¹/₂ cup sugar
1 teaspoon ground cinnamon
¹/₂ teaspoon ground cloves
¹/₄ teaspoon salt
1 cup dark corn syrup
3 large eggs
1 cup quick-cooking oatmeal

1. Preheat the oven to 350°F

2. Prepare the crust and set aside in the refrigerator while you make the filling.

3. Cream together the butter and sugar in a medium bowl. Add the cinnamon, cloves, and salt. Stir in the corn syrup. Add the eggs, 1 at a time, stirring after each addition until well blended. Stir in the oatmeal.

4. Pour the filling into the pie shell and bake in the center of the oven for 1 hour or until a knife inserted in the center comes out clean.

S E R V E S 6.

Fresh Fruit Cobblers

Cobblers were invented for harried people with a sweet tooth. Cut up any fruit on hand, dump it into a dish, top it with biscuit dough, and bake. That's it. Just remember to heat the fruit before covering it with the dough, as the dough takes less time to cook than the fruit.

Single recipe Biscuit Crust dough (page 45), unbaked

Filling:
⅔ to 1 cup sugar (depending on sweetness of fruit and your taste)
1 tablespoon cornstarch
1 cup boiling water
3 cups fresh fruit, cut into bite-size pieces
4 tablespoons (½ stick) unsalted butter
Ground cinnamon or nutmeg (or both, depending on fruit and your taste)
Heavy cream or ice cream, for serving

1. Preheat the oven to 400°F.

2. Very lightly butter a 9-inch glass or ceramic baking dish and set aside.

3. Combine the sugar and cornstarch in a medium-size heavy saucepan. Add the boiling water and stir until the sugar dissolves. Bring to a boil and boil for 1 minute.

4. Add the prepared fruit along with any juices to the saucepan; stir to coat. Pour the fruit mixture into the prepared baking dish. Dot with the butter and sprinkle with desired spices.

5. Drop spoonfuls of dough over the filling. Bake in the center of the oven for 30 minutes.

6. Serve in bowls, making sure each diner gets some of the juices. Serve with heavy cream or ice cream, if desired.

SERVES AT LEAST 6.

Cherry Clafouti

*T*his is about as easy—and delicious—as recipes come. I learned how to make this clafouti, which can be made with any fruit or berry, by watching Andrée Abramoff make it at her restaurant, Cafe Crocodile, in Manhattan. I love the way the batter forms a crust around the fruit.

Filling:
3 cups pitted cherries
3 tablespoons sugar
*$\frac{1}{4}$ to $\frac{1}{2}$ cup kirsch (depending on how strong you want
the flavor—and kick—to be)*

Batter:
$\frac{3}{4}$ cup milk
$\frac{1}{4}$ cup light cream
3 large eggs
2 teaspoons almond extract
3 tablespoons sugar
$\frac{2}{3}$ cup all-purpose flour

1. Preheat the oven to 350°F.

2. Generously butter a pie pan—preferably a glass plate so you can see the fruit—and set aside.

3. In a large bowl, combine the cherries with the sugar and kirsch. Set aside while you prepare the batter.

4. In a medium bowl, stir together all of the batter ingredients. Beat with an electric mixer (or in a food processor, using the metal blade) until smooth.

5. Pour half of the batter into the pie pan and set it in the center of the oven for about 5 minutes or until just set. Remove from the oven and top with the cherries. Spoon a tablespoon or 2 of the juice left in the bowl over the cherries. Pour in the rest of the batter.

6. Return the pan to the center of the oven and bake for 35 to 40 minutes or until the top puffs up.

7. Let cool slightly before serving.

SERVES 6 TO 8.

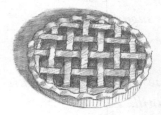
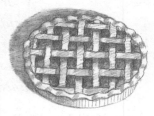

Impossible Coconut Pie

*I*mpossible pies" were a craze during the sixties, courtesy of Bisquick boxes and women's magazines. In the seventies, when my parents moved into a smaller place, they pared down their belongings to the essentials, giving away things they didn't need anymore. I got my mom's cookbooks. The pages are stuffed with neatly clipped recipes from newspapers and magazines, and it seems that every third recipe is for some kind of "impossible pie." Basically, these recipes combine crust and filling in one step. Their virtue, and I suppose the basis for their endless variety, is that you can throw a few ingredients together and with little work have a dessert or even a dinner (I remember my mom serving "impossible lasagna," though it wasn't a big hit). This impossible pie is the best, to my taste, of these miracles of modern technology.

1/2 cup self-rising flour or Bisquick
1 3/4 cups sugar
4 large eggs
2 cups milk
1 cup (2 sticks) margarine, at room temperature
2 teaspoons vanilla extract
2 cups canned flaked coconut

1. Preheat the oven to 350°F.

2. Combine the flour or Bisquick and sugar in a medium bowl, then stir in the remaining ingredients. Pour the mixture into two 8-inch pie pans.

3. Bake in the center of the oven for about 30 minutes or until a knife inserted in the center comes out clean.

EACH PIE WILL SERVE 6.

Apple Crisp

*H*ere's another quick dessert. The "crust" is actually a delicious, crunchy topping. This recipe works well with other fruits as well, such as pears or peaches.

Crust:
1 cup sugar
³/₄ cup all-purpose flour
¹/₄ cup finely chopped walnuts
7 tablespoons unsalted butter, chilled and cut into 7 pieces

Filling:
4 cups peeled apple slices, any cooking variety (see page 251)
1 teaspoon ground cinnamon
¹/₂ cup water

1. Combine the sugar, flour, and walnuts in a medium bowl. Add the butter and quickly work with your fingertips until the mixture is crumbly. Store in the refrigerator while you prepare the fruit.

2. Preheat the oven to 350°F. Butter a 6-cup casserole dish.

3. Combine the apples with the cinnamon in a large bowl, then transfer to the prepared casserole. Carefully pour the water down the side of the dish so that it nearly covers the bottom layer of apples. Spread the crust mixture over the top of the apples, patting it down firmly with the back of a spoon.

4. Bake for 30 minutes or until the apples are tender and the crust is browned.

SERVES 6.

The Children's Hour

A boy is an appetite with a skin pulled over it.

—Anonymous

When my children were small, a perfect day began—not too early—with their cheerful voices calling me from their rooms. There was breakfast and then a quick wash. Maybe we'd get dressed or maybe we'd stay in our pj's and play until *Sesame Street* came on. After that, it was nap time and as soon as they were down for the count, I'd go to my desk to write. The morning naps, even for Al, were the longest, and on those perfect days it was sometimes noon before I heard the first squawk from my children's rooms. Then we'd eat lunch and head out to the library or the park or we'd go shopping. At four o'clock we'd return, happy and tired. I'd put the kettle on, make us a little treat, and then my sons and I would settle in on the couch. I wish I could say we read all the time, but more often than not we watched cartoons or a video that we'd already seen at least a dozen times. Drugged by the activities of the long afternoon, we nestled together, comforted by the protectiveness of our entwining arms as the light faded from violet to gray through the long windows.

I can probably count on one hand the number of days that unfolded like this, but when I look back, those are the days I remember most clearly, and I still think of late afternoon as the time that belongs to children. I am not the sort of person who ever imagined herself surrounded by kids; I hated babysitting when I was growing up and though I love babies, I don't like to have them around me all the time. Yet in the afternoon, when I'm finished working, I often wander into the kitchen and find myself smack in the middle of a pack of kids. A couple are perched on the counter, another tilts a stool back against the door, and one more is twirling a basketball on the tip of his finger while a son of mine empties out the refrigerator looking for something to eat. Wading into their midst, I try not to listen to their conversations, which usually have to do with something I don't understand anyway (such as the social life and physical attributes/powers of various animated Japanese warriors). Sometimes, though, I am sidetracked by a comment and I find myself embroiled in a lively discussion on a topic that makes me long for the days of *Sesame Street*.

My children and their friends are growing up aware of situations we wish didn't exist. They know people in the neighborhood who deal drugs, some of whom go to school with them. They've seen the women who call to the cars under the elevated highway down the street. Al wonders about the old Asian woman who, with a baby strapped to her back, goes through our trash at least twice a week looking for returnable bottles; a friend's mother, as well as two close friends of ours, are wrestling with AIDS. Yet both Al and, especially, Sam complain that we protect them too much. Unlike most of their friends, they have a father who lives with them, which means there's an extra pair of eyes and another (very) vocal mouth when they're up to something they shouldn't be. We demand that they abide by rules that their companions find ridiculous, to think about moral issues and the ethics of their behavior. Still, within these parameters we have tried not to shelter them. Sam and his friends travel through the city by themselves; both boys have seen movies, read books, and listened to music that a lot of our friends find shocking. Most of this has led to good things. They are both independent, somewhat sophisticated, certainly street-wise. There have been some bad things as well. Sam has been mugged; Al has been roughed up after a stickball game on the block. We try to acknowledge both sides of the coin, without diminishing the good or glossing over the bad.

Living in the city is not easy for them; but it's often harder for some of their friends. The least I can do is let these boys linger in my kitchen and lis-ten to them when they want me to. But I'm not a fool; the sight of a room full of young, hormone-crazed teenagers and assorted younger tagalongs fills me with dread and anxiety. Whatever I was doing before their invasion is lost, the calming beauty of the late afternoon sky is dispersed. This is where having a treat on hand comes in handy—it may assure (but by no means guarantee) at least a minimum of civilized behavior.

My sister's youngest daughter lived with us last summer. An elegant, beautiful young woman, Moira grew up in a house full of women and was not used to the mysterious ways of boys. The first time she came home to find five boys surrounding the open door of our refrigerator, she started screaming and threw them all out into the backyard.

"I couldn't believe them," she complained to me later.

"What couldn't you believe?"

"That they were just standing there shoveling this whole dessert you made into their mouths. There was nothing left."

"I made it for them to do that."

"But they didn't even bother with plates. They were like a flock of vultures."

"It's okay."

"No it's not."

I drew her hair from around her face and smiled. "They were happy, weren't they?"

"They should have been."

"But they were, right?"

"Yeah."

"Then it's all right. That's what I want them to be."

"Vultures?"

"Happy," I said, and didn't expect her to understand until she was a mother herself.

NOW, I'M NOT going to pretend that the following recipes are nutritious or will ever make me a candidate for the Good Mother Award. They are, instead, simply fun—what a kid's treat ought to be. I don't recommend making any of these pies on a regular basis—unless you want your dentist to become your best friend. Think of them as legal mood-altering drugs that work not just on the patient (the kid) but on the dispenser (the parent) as well. The kid gets something special made just for him or her and the parent just may get a hug and a kiss, as well as a little peace.

Three Mile Island Pie

*T*he proper defense for this creation is that we all crave something trashy now and then. I don't know the origin of the recipe (it's probably at the bottom of a landfill somewhere), but the name was given to it by my sister's daughters, all three of whom grew up healthy and with a great appreciation for good food even though there were periods in their lives when they ate this pie at least once a week.

It is a perfect, kid-loving treat and I won't sully it by attempting to arrange the ingredients in a typical recipe format. All you need is a crumb pie crust (store-bought), a large box of Jell-O (any flavor), and a large container of Cool Whip.

Make the Jell-O using half the liquid and the quick-chill method explained on the back of the box. When the Jell-O is set, fold the Cool Whip into the cold Jell-O, then pile high into the crust. Refrigerate. (If you want to be fancy or you really need to feel something nutritious is getting into your child's body, stir chopped fruit into the Cool Whip.)

It's best to eat Three Mile Island Pie the same day you make it. The massive amount of sugar in it seems to intensify with each extra day it sits in the refrigerator.

SERVES 6 HUNGRY KIDS OR 10 POLITE ADULTS.

Banana Bundles

*T*his is not a traditional pie but gives you something to do with leftover pastry. It's as much fun to make as it is to eat.

4 bananas
¹/₃ cup sugar
Ground cinnamon to taste
Scraps left over from Butter and Lard Crust (page 25)
Ice cream or warm caramel or chocolate sauce, for serving

1. Preheat the oven to 425°F.

2. Peel the bananas, then cut in half crosswise. Roll the bananas in the sugar and sprinkle with cinnamon.

3. Combine all of the scraps of dough into a ball and quickly roll out into a ¹/₈-inch-thick sheet. Cut the dough into 8 squares that are a little bigger than the banana pieces.

4. Place each banana piece on a square of pastry and roll it up so that the banana is completely covered. Seal seam and ends with a dab of water.

5. Place each bundle on a nonstick baking sheet, seam side down. Bake in the center of the oven for 35 to 40 minutes or until the pastry is brown.

6. Serve with ice cream, warm caramel, or chocolate sauce.

SERVES 4 BIG KIDS OR 8 SMALLER KIDS.

Popcorn–Ice Cream Pie

*T*his pie has gotten me through a couple of long rainy afternoons, first because it gives me something to do with the kids and second because I make it a rule that unless they are good while we wait for the ice cream to firm up, they don't get a slice. Then we pop in a video or get a book and snuggle up on the couch with bowls of this pie in our laps.

8 cups unsalted popped popcorn
1 cup toasted, flaked coconut
1 cup sugar
8 tablespoons (1 stick) unsalted butter or margarine
¼ cup water
1 cup light corn syrup
1 teaspoon vanilla extract
1 quart child's favorite ice cream, softened
Chocolate sauce, for serving (optional)

1. Grease a large bowl with butter and pour in the popcorn and coconut. Mix together.

2. Combine the sugar, butter, water, and corn syrup in a medium-size heavy saucepan. Bring to a boil over medium heat, stirring until the sugar melts. Continue cooking and stirring until the mixture reaches the hard-ball stage (250 to 269°F on a candy thermometer). If you don't have a candy thermometer, drop a small amount of the mixture in a glass of water; if it forms a ball, it is done. When ready, remove the sugar mixture from the heat and stir in the vanilla.

3. Pour the mixture in a fine stream over the popcorn, stirring until all of the kernels are coated. Divide the mixture in half and pat into 2 greased 9-inch baking sheets or pizza pans. Set aside to cool.

4. Spread the softened ice cream over the popcorn mixture in one of the pans, then remove the popcorn mixture from the other pan and place it on top of the ice cream (the popcorn should have hardened into a crunchy layer by this point). Place the pie in the freezer until the ice cream is firm. If the ice cream is runny, wrap plastic wrap around the edges before freezing.

5. Cut into wedges to serve. Accompany with chocolate sauce, if desired.

SERVES AT LEAST 6 KIDS BUT IT STAYS GOOD
FOR A WEEK IN THE FREEZER.

Teaching Kids to Cook

One of the very few tenets of child rearing I have followed faithfully is the belief that all children need to learn how to cook. I started out both my sons early by letting them measure out ingredients and stir batters. When I am making something I know they like, I'll call them into the kitchen to show them how it's done so the next time they can do it themselves. When they want to cook something, I give them free range. I get out of the kitchen (well, I go into the next room and pretend to read) until they're done and always praise what comes out. If it's a miserable failure, I show them what went wrong and help them to make another. In this way I am assured they will be able to fend for themselves one day. Sam can now make a completely delicious dinner, and Al has mastered scrambled eggs and is moving on to pancakes and chicken wings. What's more, like the good men they're becoming, they usually remember that one of the most important parts of cooking is cleaning up afterward.

Hershey Bar Pie

Not all of these pies are made just for my children. I made this one for myself after I spent a grueling afternoon testifying against the New York City Board of Education for its failure to deal with my son's learning disability. When you've done battle with a bureaucracy, you need a potent elixir to revive you. This pie hit the spot.

Single 9-inch Basic Graham Cracker Crust (page 36), baked

Filling:
1 large (12-ounce) Hershey's almond chocolate bar
16 large, fresh marshmallows (go out and buy a new bag; don't use the ones left over from your last camping trip)
⅓ cup milk
½ cup heavy cream

1. Prepare the crust.

2. Combine all of the filling ingredients except for the heavy cream in the top of a double boiler and melt over boiling water. Do not bring the mixture to a boil! Let cool slightly.

3. Using a hand-held electric mixer, whip the cream until stiff, then add it to the chocolate mixture. Pour into the prepared pie shell and refrigerate until set—at least 2 hours.

SERVES 6.

Strawberry Parfait Pie

*B*ananas, plums, peaches, and other berries can be substituted for the straw-berries in this recipe.

Single 9-inch Basic Graham Cracker Crust (page 36)
or Granola Crust (page 37), baked

Filling:
1 small package strawberry-flavored gelatin
1¼ cups hot water
1 pint vanilla ice cream
1 pint fresh strawberries
Whipped cream, for garnish
Chocolate sauce, for serving (optional)

1. Prepare the crust.

2. In a medium bowl, dissolve the gelatin in the hot water. Add the ice cream by spoonfuls, stirring until melted. Chill until thickened but not set. Fold in the fruit and turn the mixture into the pie shell.

3. Chill until firm. Garnish with whipped cream. For an extra treat, drizzle with choco-late sauce.

SERVES 6.

Graham Cracker Pie

*T*he perfect treat for a cranky baby.

3 cups graham cracker crumbs
3 cups applesauce
Cinnamon sugar to taste

1. Press a third of the crumbs into the bottom and sides of a well-greased 9-inch pie pan. Spread half of the applesauce over the crumbs. Sprinkle with cinnamon sugar. Spread half of the remaining crumbs over the applesauce, then add a final layer of applesauce. Sprinkle with cinnamon sugar, then top with the last of the crumbs.

2. Chill for at least an hour until set.

3. To serve, place the baby in a room with washable walls and flooring. Cut out serving slices and place in a plastic bowl. Give the baby the bowl with a small spoon, then leave the table and let the baby go to town.

Serves 6. Keeps for 2 days.

Individual Mud Pies

*K*ids love the idea of getting a pie that's completely their own, and the name Mud Pie speaks to the very core of their beings. I make these pies in little tartlet tins (I found mine in a junk store near my house), but they can just as easily be made in a small cupcake pan. Just remember to lightly spray the cups with a nonstick cooking spray before lining them with pastry so that the

109

pies can be removed easily when done. This particular recipe is adapted from a book called *As Easy as Pie* by Susan Purdy.

Dough for a single 9-inch All-Butter Crust (page 26), unbaked

Filling:
8 tablespoons (1 stick) unsalted butter
2 ounces unsweetened chocolate
1 ounce semisweet chocolate
1⅓ cups sugar
3 large eggs
3 tablespoons light corn syrup
2 tablespoons sour cream
1 teaspoon vanilla extract
Vanilla yogurt, for serving (optional)

1. Preheat the oven to 350°F.

2. Carefully press the dough into the bottoms and sides of 6 individual (approximately 4-inch) tart tins or into 6 of the individual cups of a cupcake pan.

3. In the top of a double boiler over gently simmering water, melt the butter and chocolates. Set aside to cool.

4. In the bowl of a food processor fitted with the metal blade, process all of the remaining filling ingredients until well blended. Pour in the chocolate-butter mixture and pulse 4 times. Pour the batter into the prepared shells.

5. Bake in the center of the oven for 30 to 35 minutes or until the filling forms a crisp crust and the pastry edges look golden brown.

6. Let cool a bit. Serve with a dab of vanilla yogurt in the middle, if desired.

MAKES 6 TARTLETS.

Cream Cheese Tarts

*T*his is a recipe I make for Al when his big brother has picked on him too much.

12 vanilla wafers
1 (16-ounce) package cream cheese, at room temperature
$^3/_4$ cup sugar
2 large eggs
1 teaspoon vanilla extract
1 teaspoon fresh lemon juice

1. Preheat the oven to 350°F.

2. Line a 12-cup cupcake mold with paper cupcake liners and place 1 vanilla wafer at the bottom of each one. Set aside.

3. Blend the remaining ingredients together until very smooth.

4. Fill each cupcake holder until it is three-fourths full. Bake in the center of the oven for 20 to 25 minutes or until just set.

MAKES 12 TARTS

The Pleasure of
Your Company

To get the full value of joy you must have somebody to divide it with.

—MARK TWAIN, "PUDD'NHEAD WILSON'S NEW
CALENDAR," *FOLLOWING THE EQUATOR*

December always comes as a surprise to me. I'm never quite prepared for the onslaught of cheer or for the guests I invited to come over way back in the unruffled days of November. This is the time of year when pies—in all their versatility—show me their true worth and remind me, once again, why they were baked in such vast quantities in the olden days. After some bad experiences that make what Pavlov's dog went through look like a frolic, I'm conditioned now to start filling the freezer with plastic bags of pastry treats as soon as I break out the first pumpkin pie in October. By the time the real mayhem starts, any seeming grace on my part is due solely to what I know I have secreted away.

What forced me into this mode of behavior was the ever increasing attendance at our annual Christmas party. It started out as a fairly simple gathering of friends, including my oldest friend, also named Pat, who had just married her sweetheart, Mannichek; my brother, Joe; and two or three of Chris's classmates. We crowded into the living room of our small apartment, which was made even tinier by the presence of an enormous Christmas tree we'd dragged home earlier in the day. While Joe and Chris disappeared into its arms to string lights, the rest of us sat around eating bowls of chili and offering constructive criticism about the strategic placement of the bubble-lights.

I think I also made a dip. I know there was a plate of chocolate chip cookies and wreath- and star-shaped butter cookies decorated with silver sprinkles. But that was pretty much the menu. It was the first real party of our married life (the one back in Ravenna that we hosted a few days before we left for New York was just a drunken brawl). As these things go, it was pretty low key, mainly because I was seven months pregnant and just too tired (and too big) to cook anything more.

By the next year, we had moved to the top floor of an old house in Brooklyn and we actually sent out invitations. There was another gigantic Christmas tree that dwarfed one of our four rooms, but there were many more people and the spread I put out was much more extravagant. I made an assortment of dumplings; pakoras (Indian vegetable fritters); a goat cheese spread; a large platter of lamb curry surrounded by different chutneys and basmati rice; and, for dessert, a tower of floating islands in raspberry sauce, a large trifle, chocolate mousse cake, and a lemon tart, not to mention the usual array of Christmas cookies. From that year on, the Christmas party just got bigger and bigger. Each year we crowded more and more people into the Brooklyn apartment and later into our ramshackle house, and the food I served grew as complicated and intricate as a Chinese magic trick.

I've come to believe that what Chris and I have been doing all these years is to try and push our way through our parents' style of party-giving in order to find our own. No one gives a party by themselves; even in the fledgling wildness of a person's first hosted party there lurks in the background filmy apparitions of family gatherings from childhood. This is why for my first party I felt a sudden urge to stick flowers in an empty wine bottle and set it down among the bowls of potato chips. This is why at her first dinner party a friend of mine was compelled to put out those little dinner mints in crinkly paper envelopes even though they were the last thing her guests wanted after the spaghetti dinner she'd served.

It was natural for me, as my mother's daughter, to think I had to provide a lavish table of food and drinks. On rare occasions, my mom would buy a container of prepared food, but she always, in her words, "doctored it up," which meant she added spices and herbs, maybe a little Worcestershire sauce or ketchup. She could transform what she'd bought into something totally different—and much better tasting—than what it had been when it left the store.

Every table in my parents' house would be brimming with things to eat, from an arrangement of dips, olives, and spicy nuts in the living room to the chafing dishes and overflowing platters on the dining room table. The long counter in the kitchen would be jammed with dishes in the final stages of preparation, waiting for a frill of parsley or a dusting of pepper before they were sent to the dining room to do their work. My mother stood at the stove and calculated, by the sounds in the next room, when to present each dish to best advantage. Experienced guests knew that the best place to stand was right outside the kitchen door so they could see what was coming and be the first to taste it. Others roosted on the long windowsill beside the dining room table, while more adventurous souls darted from room to room like sandpipers, picking quickly at a new dish here then falling back to find another one there.

After dessert was offered and coffee was poured, the guests migrated toward the kitchen, where the last tasty crumbs of the meal could be picked through. The women sat at the kitchen table around my mother; the men gravitated with my father to the laundry room, where the bar was arranged on top of the dryer and the beer was packed in the ice-filled washing machine. The children bounced from one group to the other, pressed into service by the men to deliver drinks to the women, only to be sent back by one of the women to repeat a rejoinder to something they overheard the men saying. Very late at night, tongues loosened with drink, the presence of children all but forgotten, the men and women melted together around the kitchen table to exchange stories about the past, spinning out tales of strife and endurance, loyalty and love.

The parties Chris's family gave were something different. In the early years of Chris's life, when rock 'n' roll was just breaking out, his father, Joe, was one of the top radio disc jockeys in the country. The Cleveland station where Joe worked was an important venue for records climbing the charts. Record company executives courted him and the other disc jockeys with all the weapons in their wealthy arsenals. In return, Chris's dad, at the age of twenty-three, became something of a celebrity and, before the first payola scandal broke, his family lived a rather swell life. We have a great photograph of my mother-in-law clipped from a newspaper society page. She's dressed in a tight-waisted brocade-and-lace hostess gown, complete with a *train*. She has a dramatic white streak in her dark, cropped hair, a cigarette holder in her raised hand, and a cocktail glass on the table beside her. The caption reads, "Mrs. Finan, at home for the holidays, awaits her guests."

There were some family parties, but my in-laws also did a great deal of business entertaining. Chris's father invited everyone he met at work—from musicians to executives—"back to the house" for drinks or dinner. Chris's mom, however, had no love of cooking and, in fact, had no real interest in food that I could detect, so she relied on caterers and specialty stores. She would put some macadamia nuts in silver bowls and place them on tables here and there. The meal would start with, perhaps, a pâté, followed by a ham and maybe some fancy cookies with ice cream for dessert. Perfectly acceptable, especially, as she pointed out to me once, when most of your guests are tanked. What kept the guests happy was the lively atmosphere Chris's parents created. Former theater students, they both were well read, politically involved, and told stories with great style. Their parties went on until the wee hours of the morning, fueled by a seemingly endless supply of liquor, spirited discussion, and lots of generous laughter.

In our early years together, Chris and I gave parties that fell somewhere in between these two styles. We weren't glamorous like his parents and we were gradually backing away from the whiskey-fueled cadence of mine. Nevertheless, we continued to emulate bits of our parents' styles at our annual Christmas party. For Chris, it meant inviting everyone he came to know and like throughout the year. For me, I just kept cooking, adding one more laborious dish after another until I was starting to prepare for the party in September. To get to our party, people drove for hours, through snowstorms and gales; friends brought friends; guests spent the night; every bed, couch, and rug was taken up by a snoring body. After a while I stopped counting how many guests were expected and began simply to plan for a sizable army. One year when there was a very bad storm and only a third of the usual suspects showed up, I discovered an interesting fact: it didn't matter how much food I prepared or how many guests arrived, the same meager scraps were left behind.

It took us at least eight Christmas parties—and the physical breakdowns that followed them—to get it exactly right. Chris doesn't invite so many people anymore and he's more inclined to enjoy his guests rather than perform for them like his father did. I admit, though, it's taken me a little longer to break away from my mother's rather compulsive, I've-got-to-do-it-all-myself entertainment style. As I've gotten older, as life has lost its simplicity (or I have gotten saner), I've been forced to take a few lessons from my gracious mother-in-law. A few years ago I ordered my first honey-baked ham and its success squashed all my guilt about serving something I had not even "doctored up." I couldn't control the need to make some biscuits and a chutney or

Martha and Me

Last summer we went on vacation with Chris's dad and I became addicted to *Martha Stewart Living* magazine. My father-in-law rented a house—a much more upscale version of the beach houses we usually can afford—and the woman who owned it had stacks of the magazine around. I had never seen the magazine before, but once I opened an issue I was hooked. I loved the idea of "unsweetened" pumpkin–colored walls and of marking my stationery and wrapping paper with potato stamps. I did almost nothing that week but read those magazines, marking the projects I was going to embark on as soon as I got home. I saw my house, my children—indeed, my life—projected in an amber light of what they could become.

Reality slapped me silly once I came home. I had filled out a subscription card and mailed it from the shore, but within two months I was sick of controlled perfection. I wasn't sure who the magazine was for, but I knew it wasn't for me. Even the ideas I found intriguing (substituting screens for glass in cabinet doors, for instance) turned out to be too expensive ($8/square *inch* for the copper screen Martha recommends) or too time-consuming. I canceled my subscription and chalked up my momentary fixation to a summertime delusion brought on by the heat of the sun.

And yet I learned a lot about the particular subject of entertaining from Martha. In that realm, she espouses a very sensible style that I find civilized. Maybe it's because we both need more therapy, but like Martha, I starch and iron the tablecloths I drape over the dining table and the library table I use as a bar. It is, however, the only time I starch and iron anything, and the cloths cover tables that are less than perfect. I don't carve vegetables and fruits into flowers or bowls, but I have used them in their natural state as a centerpiece or on the mantel in place of flowers. They're often cheaper than the carnations for sale in my neighborhood. Before guests come, I put drops of perfume on the lightbulbs. Martha may do it just for the fragrance—I usually do it because one of the dogs needs a bath. Certainly Martha's guests wouldn't be as impressed by my house as they are by hers, but I'm sure they would find a level of conviviality they would equally enjoy.

two to go with it, but that was a step in a more rational direction than trying to make the entire meal myself. The time it saved was such a blessed relief that I began to look for other ways to shorten the marathon of cooking I had felt doomed, as my mother's daughter, to run.

That's where pies come in. The fact that you can freeze dough for a few months and encase anything in it makes pies perfect for mass gatherings. Hors d'oeuvres are particularly well suited to this kind of preparation. Great hors d'oeuvres are the best weapon in a party giver's arsenal. They set the tempo for the evening, getting the hungry guests in the mood for what lies ahead. More importantly, they also provide a cushion of time. The hosts can catch their breath and even sit down with a peaceful drink before the onslaught begins. When all the guests finally arrive and coats and bags are put away, an offering of these little gems puts people immediately at ease. Munching on delicious bite-size treats, the guests begin to circulate and soon you have a happy assembly that is slowly revving up into higher and higher gear.

For a large party, try to have at least three or four different kinds of hors d'oeuvres on hand. The variety of tastes will promote even more circulation among the guests as they seek out what they haven't yet tasted. The pastry that hors d'oeuvres require is probably the simplest of all to make and you can improvise fillings out of almost anything you have on hand, from ground nuts to smoked fish. I keep packages of phyllo dough, dumpling skins, and empanada wrappers in the freezer because they not only make terrific casings but they come to the rescue if we have a surge of unexpected guests or I'm having a kitchen emergency and the main meal is going to be delayed. One year, when I came down with the flu two weeks before the party and was too dazed to do the usual amount of cooking, I made do with just appetizers and desserts, the two parts of the meal I had already prepared. When we ran out, I enlisted the help of a couple of guests and we started turning out little dumplings and phyllo triangles stuffed with ingredients we found in the refrigerator and cabinets. Most were combinations I never would have thought of (for example, leftover roast pork ground with dried apricots and walnuts, moistened with a little Canadian whiskey), and the evening turned out to be one of the most enjoyable—and memorable—of all the Christmas parties.

A FEW DAYS before Thanksgiving I usually make one or two of the recipes in this chapter. If the hors d'oeuvres I choose call for baking, I sometimes do even that in advance, so that all I have to do at the party is heat them up. Otherwise, I wrap each batch in plastic wrap or throw them into baggies, then toss them into the freezer with a label to remind me what they are. I always start out thinking I'm going to make many different kinds but usually end up with something like three or four varieties. Even that's probably a little ridiculous, but the closer we get to the holidays, the more generous I feel. When I'm thinking about what to serve, I try to make sure that the flavors of the hors d'oeuvres complement the overall meal I have planned. I also like to prepare an hors d'oeuvre that's spicy, another that's soothing, and another that's just plain exquisite. That doesn't mean caviar—half the people we hang out with would think we were putting on airs; the other half probably wouldn't recognize it and would wonder if I had accidentally opened a can of pet food. Instead, it might be something like an elegant cheese or a more expensive shellfish, little treasures that make our friends feel pampered and the holidays feel special.

I've separated the party recipes into three groups: the first group calls for pastry, the second, phyllo dough, and the third, wrappers for dumplings and empanadas. The different fillings listed under each can be interchanged, though it is important to keep in mind the differences in taste among the three kinds of dough. For instance, the tart shells have a delicate buttery flavor that doesn't go very well with a highly seasoned filling. Phyllo dough and wrappers are blander and can take—and sometimes even demand—a spicier filling. The dipping sauces listed at the end of the chapter can be used with phyllo, dumplings, or empanadas. Unless you're a glutton for spices, try not to couple a spicy dip with an equally spicy filling. It's overkill.

Pastry

*T*he pastry called for in most of the following recipes is the Savory Tart Crust on page 41. I will sometimes make a great batch of this dough, cut it into several portions, and freeze it in plastic bags. I can then rely on it in a hurry when friends stop in. As Chris takes coats and settles everyone in, I run to the kitchen, grab a bag of dough, and throw it into the microwave for a minute or two on high. Then, while the coffee is brewing, I roll the dough out, fit it into a pan, and come up with a filling from whatever I have on hand. Instead of freezing dough, it is also possible to freeze empty shells. Wrapped tightly in plastic or stacked in airtight containers in the freezer, they will keep for up to six weeks. Defrost slowly in the refrigerator before filling them.

Tartlets are tiny saucers of flavor. You can make them any size you wish—out of the very small molds for sale at cooking specialty stores or in regular cupcake molds (my sister uses the cupcake mold one of her daughters got in a play kitchen set). The small molds make hors d'oeuvres that are just big enough for your guests to pop into their mouths in one bite; if you use a regular cupcake mold, layer the pastry only halfway up the sides.

Red Pepper Caviar Tartlets

Double recipe Savory Tart Crust tartlet shells (page 41), baked

Filling:
8 pounds large red bell peppers
$^2/_3$ cup olive oil
$1^1/_2$ teaspoons salt
1 teaspoon dried thyme
$^1/_4$ to $^1/_2$ teaspoon ground red pepper (to taste)
$^1/_4$ cup imported, shredded Swiss cheese

1. Prepare the tartlet shells.

2. Slice the red peppers into thin strips, removing all the seeds and ribs.

3. Heat the oil in an 8-quart stockpot over medium heat. Stir in the pepper slices, then add the salt, thyme, and ground red pepper. Cover and simmer until very soft, stirring occasionally, about 1 hour.

4. Drain the peppers completely. Transfer to the bowl of a food processor fitted with the metal blade and purée until smooth, scraping down the bowl as necessary (you may have to do this in batches). Press the purée through a fine sieve to remove any bits of skin.

5. Fill the baked tartlet shells with the red pepper mixture and sprinkle the grated cheese over the top. Place under the broiler for 1 to 2 minutes, until the cheese melts. Serve at once.

MAKES ABOUT 48 STANDARD-SIZE TARTLETS
OR 72 MINI TARTLETS.

Onion-Apple Tartlets

Savory Tart Crust tartlet shells (page 41), unbaked

Filling:

4 ounces lean bacon, coarsely chopped

4 medium onions, sliced into thin rounds

1 large, very tart apple, peeled, cored, and thinly sliced

$\frac{1}{2}$ teaspoon caraway seeds

$\frac{1}{2}$ teaspoon chopped fresh chives

4 ounces Gruyère cheese, shredded

4 ounces Emmentaler cheese, shredded

2 large eggs

1 cup milk

3 tablespoons sour cream

Large pinch paprika

Salt and freshly ground black pepper to taste

1. Preheat the oven to 350°F.

2. Prepare the tartlet shells and place in the refrigerator while you make the filling.

3. In a medium frying pan, sauté the bacon bits until slightly cooked and the fat is rendered. Remove the bacon with a slotted spoon and drain on a paper towel. Cook the onions over low heat in the bacon fat, stirring constantly, until soft, about 15 to 20 minutes.

4. Stir the apple slices into the onions and sauté for about 5 minutes. Add the bacon, caraway seeds, and chives.

5. Combine the two shredded cheeses in a small bowl.

6. In a separate bowl, combine the eggs, milk, sour cream, paprika, and salt and pepper.

7. Spoon the onion-apple mixture into the shells and sprinkle half of the cheese on top. Pour the egg mixture over the cheese layer and top with the remaining cheese.

8. Bake in the center of the oven for 15 minutes. Raise the oven temperature to 425°F and bake until the tartlets are bubbling brown, about 10 to 15 minutes more. Let cool to room temperature and serve on pretty napkins or doilies.

MAKES ABOUT 24 STANDARD-SIZE TARTLETS
OR 36 MINI TARTLETS.

Herbed Goat Cheese Tartlets

Savory Tart Crust tartlet shells (page 41), baked

Filling:
1 small log (about 4 ounces) high-quality goat cheese,
at room temperature
3 tablespoons unsalted butter, at room temperature
1 tablespoon herbes de Provence
$1/4$ teaspoon freshly ground black pepper

1. Prepare the tartlet shells.

2. Combine all of the ingredients in the bowl of a food processor fitted with the metal blade and process until smooth.

3. Divide the filling among the baked tart shells. Serve as is or heated under the broiler for about 2 minutes. Watch carefully to avoid burning.

MAKES ABOUT 24 STANDARD-SIZE TARTLETS
OR 36 MINI TARTLETS.

Tapénade Tartlets

Savory Tart Crust tartlet shells (page 41), baked

Filling:
1 cup pitted black olives, coarsely chopped
1 tablespoon minced garlic
1 tablespoon drained capers
1 can (2 ounces) anchovies, well drained
Good-quality olive oil
Crumbled blue cheese

1. Prepare the tartlet shells.

2. Combine all of the ingredients except for the oil and blue cheese in the bowl of a food processor fitted with the metal blade and process just until the mixture begins to look smooth. Scrape into a bowl and stir in olive oil by hand, a little at a time, until you have a pretty smooth paste. This creates a coarser tapénade than is customary but it's better with the pastry shells.

3. Divide the filling among the baked tart shells. Just before serving, lightly sprinkle blue cheese over the top and pass under the broiler for 1 minute. Serve warm.

MAKES ABOUT 24 STANDARD-SIZE TARTLETS
OR 36 MINI TARTLETS.

Crabmeat Tartlets

Savory Tart Crust tartlet shells (page 41), baked

Filling:
2 small lobster tails, cooked and shelled, meat finely chopped
8 generous tablespoons cooked, shredded crabmeat,
picked over to remove any small bits of shell
3 large hard-boiled eggs, minced
3 tablespoons minced onion
2 teaspoons minced garlic
Salt and freshly ground black pepper to taste
Juice from 1 large lime
Approximately $\frac{1}{2}$ cup mayonnaise
Fresh cilantro, for garnish

1. Prepare the tartlet shells.

2. Combine all of the ingredients except for the cilantro in a bowl and stir until smooth, adding just enough mayonnaise to bind the ingredients together. Just before serving, spoon the filling into the baked shells and garnish each tartlet with one small cilantro leaf or sprig.

MAKES ABOUT 24 STANDARD-SIZE TARTLETS
OR 36 MINI TARTLETS.

Roquefort Tartlets

Savory Tart Crust tartlet shells (page 41), baked

Filling:

6 ounces Roquefort cheese, at room temperature

3 ounces cream cheese, at room temperature

³⁄₄ cup heavy cream

4 large eggs

Freshly ground black pepper to taste

1. Prepare the tartlet shells.

2. Preheat the oven to 375°F.

3. Combine all of the ingredients except the pepper in the bowl of a food processor fitted with the metal blade and process until smooth. Season with the pepper.

4. Divide the filling among the shells and bake for 35 to 40 minutes or until the filling puffs up golden. Serve while still warm.

MAKES ABOUT 24 STANDARD-SIZE TARTLETS

OR 36 MINI TARTLETS.

Filling Ingredients You May Have on Hand

I f a crew of people suddenly materializes on your doorstep and you've run out of fillings, don't panic. Open up your refrigerator and cabinets and root around for something creative you might have on hand. Here are a few of the fillings I've discovered when under the gun.

Refried Beans: Use one 12-ounce can, processed briefly in the food processor until smooth and livened up with the addition of chopped garlic and jalapeño peppers to taste. Fill baked shells and place under the broiler for a minute or 2. Dab some sour cream and thinly sliced scallions on the tops before serving.

Pesto: Spread on the bottom of the baked shells.

Sun-Dried Tomatoes, Roasted Peppers, or Marinated Eggplant: Shred and drizzle with fine-quality olive oil.

Smoked-Fish Spread: Process flaked, boned, smoked fish (such as salmon, trout, bluefish, or mackerel) in the bowl of a food processor fitted with the metal blade. Add heavy cream in a stream until smooth.

Cottage Cheese and Minced Garlic: Whip until smooth with a small quantity of heavy cream. Serve at room temperature or heat briefly under a broiler.

Thinly Sliced Fresh Tomatoes: Sprinkle with olive oil, fresh thyme, oregano, and mozzarella cheese.

Spicy Shrimp Tart

This is a very rich dish. Instead of making tartlets, use a tart pan with a removable bottom.

Single 11-inch Savory Tart Crust (page 41),
partially baked

Filling:
2 tablespoons olive oil
1 tablespoon unsalted butter
1 small onion, finely chopped
1 clove garlic, finely chopped
$^1\!/_4$ teaspoon ground red pepper
1 teaspoon Tabasco
$^1\!/_2$ cup dry white wine
1 pound medium shrimp, heads removed
$2^1\!/_4$ cups heavy cream
3 large eggs
2 large egg yolks

1. Prepare the crust.

2. Preheat the oven to 350°F.

3. Cook the oil and butter in a large skillet over medium heat until the butter is melted. Add the onion and garlic and sauté until the onion is translucent. Add the ground red pepper and Tabasco, then raise the heat to high and add the wine. Continue to cook, stirring the vegetables, until the liquid is reduced by half, about 5 minutes. Remove from the heat and set aside.

4. Fill a medium saucepan with water and bring to a boil. Add the shrimp and cook until they turn pink. Drain and set aside to cool. Remove the shells from the shrimp, reserving the shells. Set aside 6 or 8 shrimp. Coarsely chop the rest of the shrimp and set aside.

5. In a food processor fitted with the metal blade, coarsely chop the shrimp shells with the onion mixture. With the motor running, pour $\frac{1}{4}$ cup of the cream through the feed tube. Process until smooth, stopping once to scrape down the sides of the bowl. Pour the shrimp-shell mixture into a sieve placed over a bowl. With the back of a spoon, press the mixture through the sieve to remove as much liquid as you can. Discard the shrimp-shell mixture that's left in the sieve.

6. Pour the shrimp liquid in the bowl into the processor and process with the remaining cream, the eggs, and egg yolks. Fold the mixture into the diced shrimp, then pour the filling into the prepared tart shell. Arrange the reserved shrimp around the top in a pinwheel design.

7. Bake the tart in the middle of the oven for about 40 minutes or until a knife inserted into the center comes out clean. Let stand for a few minutes, then cut into slices and serve warm.

SERVES 6 TO 8 AS A FIRST COURSE,
UP TO 12 FOR APPETIZERS IF THINLY SLICED.

Tomato and Goat Cheese Tart

At the end of the summer, if I've had a good crop of tomatoes, I freeze my sur-plus, anticipating this tart. I remove the leaves and stems, wash the tomatoes, and place them whole (some people prefer to remove the seeds and skin) in seal-able plastic bags. When I make this tart in the dead of winter with the last of the summer tomatoes, it reminds me of eating outdoors in our wild little yard, and the kids throwing a baseball precariously close to my head.

Single 11-inch Savory Tart Crust (page 41), unbaked

Filling:
6 medium tomatoes
1 cup fresh basil leaves, plus extra sprigs for garnish
3 large cloves garlic, chopped
¼ cup olive oil
1½ tablespoons grated Parmesan cheese
1 large egg, lightly beaten
4 ounces goat cheese, at room temperature

1. Prepare the tart dough, shape into a disk, and place in the refrigerator while you make the filling.

2. Remove the cores and seeds from the tomatoes and coarsely chop the flesh. Place the chopped tomatoes in a bowl, sprinkle them with a little salt, and let stand for an hour.

3. Preheat the oven to 425°F.

4. In a food processor fitted with the metal blade, process the basil with the gar-lic. With the motor running, pour the olive oil through the feed tube until you have a paste. Scrape the mixture into a bowl and add the Parmesan cheese.

5. Roll the tart dough out on a lightly floured surface. Roll into either a long rectangle (if making the tart on a baking sheet) or a circle (if using a pizza pan). Don't worry if the dough doesn't reach the edges of the baking sheet. Transfer the dough to the pan and fold the edges up to form a border. Brush the surface with the beaten egg. Refrigerate for 30 minutes, then bake for about 10 to 12 minutes or until lightly browned. Cool on a wire rack.

6. Combine the goat cheese with two-thirds of the basil sauce. Spread the goat cheese over the dough. Arrange the tomatoes on top, covering as much of the cheese as you can. Return to the oven for 7 more minutes or until the filling puffs up slightly.

7. Spoon the remaining basil sauce over the tomatoes and garnish with fresh basil sprigs. Cut into serving pieces.

SERVES 6 TO 8.

Little Pork Pies

The landlord of the house we lived in when we first moved to Brooklyn was a Peruvian Indian, and his wife was a Mexican Indian. They lived downstairs from us and occasionally they invited us to eat with them. Mrs. Quinonis was one of the finest cooks I've ever known and, like most great cooks, she waved off any compliments I gave her. We were both so terribly shy and respectful of the other's privacy that I could never bring myself to ask her if I could watch her cook.

Early one summer Sunday soon after we moved in, I stood at our back window and watched Mr. Quinonis and his brothers pave a small section of the backyard with quarry tiles, then build a sturdy, planked table that was beautiful in its simplicity. As the bright yellow fingers of sunlight raked through the apple and pear trees, Mrs. Quinonis carried out a tray of little pies. I couldn't make out exactly what they were at the time, but later she told me that they were one of her husband's favorite foods and that she always made them when he was doing something for her for which she was grateful. That Sunday, the men put down their hammers and washed their hands under the garden hose, sprayed their thick muscular necks and shoulders with the cool water, then sat down around the newly made table. Bottles of cold beer were opened and raised up in a salute before the men dove into the first of the many platters Mrs. Quinonis brought out to them. Their voices, the musical beauty of highland Peru, drifted up to me with the first of the summer's fireflies, and as I stood at the window with my son asleep on my shoulder, I was so happy to have found a home in which people so openly enjoyed themselves.

The crust—which is strong and bready in consistency—is used only for these pies.

Crust:
1 teaspoon active dry yeast
2 tablespoons warm water
1³/₄ cups sifted all-purpose flour
1 large egg, lightly beaten
¹/₂ cup warm milk
1 tablespoon unsalted butter, melted

Filling:
¹/₂ pound lean pork
1¹/₂ tablespoons olive oil
1 cup grated onion (save juice)
2 large cloves garlic, minced
¹/₄ cup chopped, skinned tomato
¹/₄ to ¹/₂ teaspoon saffron threads
Salt to taste
Olive oil, for frying

1. To make the crust, dissolve the yeast in the water and let stand until it bubbles. In a medium bowl, mix the flour with the egg until well incorporated, then add the milk and melted butter. Mix quickly, then add the yeast. Turn the dough out onto a lightly floured surface and briefly knead until smooth and not sticky.

2. Place the dough in a bowl lightly greased with butter, turning to coat. Cover with a towel and leave in a warm place until doubled in size, about 1 hour.

3. To make the filling, in a food processor fitted with the metal blade, chop the pork until very fine.

4. Heat the 1¹/₂ tablespoons olive oil in a skillet over medium heat. Add the onion with its juice and the garlic and sauté until the onion is just golden

brown. Add the meat and cook, stirring until the meat is cooked through. Stir in the tomato, saffron, and salt, reduce the heat to low, and cook for 5 minutes. Set aside.

5. To assemble the pies, punch down the dough and divide into balls that are about 1 inch in diameter. On a lightly floured surface, roll the pieces of dough into circles (you can make perfect circles by using a biscuit cutter).

6. In the center of each circle place about a tablespoon of filling and flatten it a little (in other words, don't mound it). Pull the sides up around the filling and pinch to seal. You may want to use some water along the edges if the dough isn't sticking together. These pies should look like little Hershey's Kisses with a knot of dough on top.

7. Heat the oil for frying in a clean skillet or wok until it's very hot. Carefully lower each pie into the oil with a slotted spoon and fry, turning frequently, until puffed up and golden, about 5 minutes.

8. Remove the pies with the slotted spoon, drain well, and serve while still slightly warm.

M A K E S   A B O U T   A   D O Z E N   P I E S

Bouchées

Okay, these are not pies, but they are made with pâte à choux. The dough is piped around the filling with a pastry bag, which makes it look like you meticulously stuffed each and every elegant little puff. These are very simple to make and freeze beautifully.

Single recipe Pâte à Choux (page 44), unbaked

Filling of your choice (recipes follow)

1. Preheat the oven to 450°F.

2. Prepare the pastry and refrigerate while you make the filling of your choice.

3. Using a teaspoon, mound the filling on a lightly oiled baking sheet about 1 inch apart.

4. Fill a pastry bag fitted with a medium tip about three-quarters of the way to the top with the pâte à choux. Pipe the pastry in overlapping circles around each mound of filling until the filling is almost completely covered. Leave a little opening at the top.

5. Bake in the center of the oven for 8 minutes. Reduce the heat to 400°F and bake another 6 to 8 minutes or until the pastry is browned. Cool on a wire rack.

6. Serve the bouchées immediately or freeze them (tightly wrapped, they'll keep for several months). To reheat, bake the frozen bouchées at 375°F for about 8 minutes.

MAKES ABOUT 80 SMALL HORS D'OEUVRES.

Use the following bouchée fillings, one each for seafood, meat, and cheese, as a guide to creating your own. For instance, you can substitute fish (such as smoked or fresh salmon, sole, or trout) for the seafood and chicken or turkey for the meat. Make a particularly interesting variation by replacing the cheese with puréed and seasoned beans, such as black beans, chickpeas, or Italian white beans.

Seafood Filling

1 small onion
2 cloves garlic
1 cup cooked bay scallops
1 cup cooked small, shelled shrimp
8 tablespoons (1 stick) unsalted butter, at room temperature
2 teaspoons fresh lemon juice
4 or 5 drops Louisiana hot sauce
1 teaspoon fresh thyme ($\frac{1}{2}$ teaspoon dried)

1. In the bowl of a food processor fitted with the metal blade, chop the onion and garlic until finely minced. Add the remaining ingredients and process until smooth. Taste and correct seasoning.

Meat Filling

11 ounces cooked pork or beef fillet, cut into cubes
8 tablespoons (1 stick) unsalted butter, at room temperature
1 small onion
8 anchovy fillets, well drained and rinsed
2 cloves garlic
1½ teaspoons herbes de Provence
Salt and freshly ground black pepper to taste

1. In the bowl of a food processor fitted with the metal blade, process all of the ingredients until you have a fairly smooth paste. Scrape down the bowl as necessary.

Cheese Filling

3 medium shallots
8 ounces wild mushrooms
4 tablespoons (½ stick) unsalted butter
4 ounces Gruyère cheese
1 large egg
Pinch of strong Hungarian paprika

1. In the bowl of a food processor fitted with the metal blade, process the shallots and mushrooms until finely chopped. Melt the butter in a skillet, add the mushroom mixture, and sauté over medium heat for about 10 minutes. Set aside to cool.

2. Process the cheese in the processor until coarsely chopped. Add the egg and paprika and pulse a few times. Stir the cheese into the mushroom mixture.

Phyllo

My sister taught me about phyllo. In the early eighties she was a member of a baking club—a loosely organized bunch of women who, at the time, were staying home having babies while their husbands renovated their homes during the evening and on weekends. As plaster dust snowed down around them, these women sought refuge in their kitchens, turning out one grandiose concoction after another. I thought of what they made as a barometer for their state of mind: anybody who spends hours seriously constructing a miniature Christmas village out of spun sugar is someone who is avoiding life. I still believe this. But they did cook up some marvelous dishes, and I was glad to eat anything they made when I visited my sister. Once the club gave a cocktail party. The women met at an appointed house (the one that happened to be the furthest along in its renovations) and prepared all kinds of hors d'oeuvres. Then they ran home, changed into a fancy dress, made their husbands put on a suit, then returned and stood around munching on hors d'oeuvres and working their way through things like stingers, sidecars, and Rob Roys.

My sister created the filling recipes that follow. For a refresher course on working with phyllo, turn to page 48. Unless noted otherwise, cook phyllo pastries at 375°F in a preheated oven for 10 to 12 minutes or until the top is puffy and golden. Let rest for 5 to 10 minutes, then cut into serving-pieces. Each recipe will yield enough filling for approximately 24 triangles, about 1 inch on each side.

Mashed Sweet Potato Filling

Combine mashed sweet potatoes with a dash of Tabasco sauce and chili powder.

Ratatouille Filling

2 tablespoons olive oil
1 small onion, chopped
1 small green bell pepper, chopped
2 medium zucchini, chopped
1 medium eggplant, peeled and chopped
2 cloves garlic, finely chopped
Salt and freshly ground black pepper to taste
Dried thyme to taste

1. Heat the oil in a large skillet over medium heat. Add the vegetables and garlic and sauté until the vegetables begin to soften and the garlic is tawny brown. Add the salt, pepper, and thyme to taste. Continue cooking over low heat until the vegetables are soft and their flavors have melded together (at least an hour).

Spinach and Goat Cheese Filling

4 tablespoons (¹/₂ stick) unsalted butter
1 cup chopped walnuts
1 large shallot, thinly sliced
2 cloves garlic, chopped
1 teaspoon dried thyme
1 teaspoon dried rosemary
Salt and freshly ground black pepper to taste
¹/₄ cup white wine
1 large bunch fresh spinach, well washed and shredded
8 ounces goat cheese
¹/₂ cup plain yogurt
¹/₄ cup grated Parmesan cheese
2 large eggs, beaten

1. Preheat the oven to 400°F.

2. Melt 2 tablespoons of the butter in a large skillet. Add the walnut pieces and sauté over medium heat until slightly softened. Set aside. Melt the rest of the butter in the skillet, then add the shallot and garlic and sauté for about 2 minutes. Add the thyme, rosemary, salt, pepper, and wine and continue cooking until the shallots are soft. Add the spinach, toss gently with the shallots, and cook just until the spinach is wilted.

3. Scrape the vegetables into a medium bowl, then add the goat cheese, yogurt, Parmesan cheese, and eggs. Mix well.

4. Scatter half of the walnuts on the bottom layer of phyllo, then top them with the spinach mixture. Sprinkle the rest of the walnuts on top of the spinach

before adding the top layers of phyllo. Score the top with diagonal cuts to make diamond shapes, then cook for 40 minutes or until brown.

Ginger-Cauliflower Filling

2-inch piece fresh ginger, peeled and coarsely chopped
$\frac{1}{2}$ cup olive oil
$\frac{1}{2}$ teaspoon ground turmeric
1 jalapeño pepper, finely chopped
1 cup loosely packed fresh cilantro leaves
1 large head cauliflower, florets removed from the stems
and sliced into small pieces
1 tablespoon fresh lemon juice
2 teaspoons ground coriander
1 teaspoon ground cumin
Salt to taste

1. In the bowl of a food processor fitted with the metal blade, blend the ginger with about 2 tablespoons water until the mixture is smooth. Set aside.

2. Heat the oil in a large skillet. Add the ginger paste and turmeric and fry over medium-high heat for 1 minute. Add the jalapeño pepper and cilantro leaves and cook for another minute, then add the cauliflower and cook for about 5 minutes. Add the remaining ingredients and 3 to 5 tablespoons water if the mixture seems dry. Taste a bit and add more salt if needed. Cover the skillet and cook for about 15 minutes, until the cauliflower is cooked through but still on the crisp side. Drain any liquid from the cauliflower before using it as a filling.

Smoked Eggplant Filling

This is a Middle Eastern recipe I got from a friend of mine who married a wonderful Iranian man who loves to eat. Shortly after they got married, his mother came over and stayed with them for several months in order to teach my friend how to cook for her son. They live in Cleveland and whenever we visit them, she serves this dish.

1 large eggplant
1 medium onion, coarsely chopped
2-inch piece fresh ginger, peeled and coarsely chopped
2 cloves garlic
5 tablespoons vegetable oil
1 teaspoon ground turmeric
2 tablespoons chopped fresh cilantro leaves
3 Italian plum tomatoes, coarsely chopped
Juice of 1 lemon
Salt to taste

1. If you have a gas stove, line the burner with aluminum foil and turn the flame to medium. Place the eggplant on top of the flame and leave it there but watch it carefully. When the skin begins to blister, turn it to another side. Keep doing this until the entire surface of the eggplant is blistered. If you have an electric stove, broil the eggplant, watching it carefully and turning it often until the skin is blistered all around. Watch your hands; use tongs or a long fork to move the eggplant. When the eggplant is done, carry it as best you can to the sink and run it under cold water. Peel the blackened skin from the pulp. Shake off as much water as you can, then coarsely chop the pulp. Set aside.

2. In the bowl of a food processor fitted with the metal blade, process the onion, ginger, and garlic with about 3 tablespoons water. Blend until a thick paste forms.

3. Heat the oil in a medium skillet over medium heat. Pour the paste into the skillet and add the turmeric. Cook for about 5 minutes or until the mixture begins to turn brown. Add the cilantro and then the tomatoes. Stir for 1 minute, then add the eggplant. Raise the heat and cook for 10 minutes, stirring constantly, until the mixture thickens to a paste. Remove from the heat and season with lemon juice and salt.

Beef Wellington Filling

8 to 12 ounces raw filet mignon
2 to 3 tablespoons unsalted butter
4 ounces porcini mushrooms, sliced into small,
thin slivers (see Note)
Salt and freshly ground black pepper to taste

1. Preheat the oven to 375°F.

2. Slice the beef into small finger-shaped, bite-size pieces and set aside. (If you like your meat well done, sauté the beef briefly in a tablespoon of butter until brown.)

3. Melt 2 tablespoons of the butter in a medium skillet. Add the mushrooms and sauté over medium-high heat until they wilt. Add more butter if needed. Season to taste with salt and pepper.

4. Layer 4 sheets of phyllo dough, brushing melted butter between each one. Cut the sheets lengthwise into 3-inch-wide strips, then cut the strips in half crosswise. Place a damp towel over the strips.

5. Remove one of the strips from under the towel. Place a piece of beef at the bottom of the short side of the strip, then top the meat with about $\frac{1}{2}$ teaspoon of the mushroom mixture. Fold one end of the phyllo on an angle up over the top of the meat and mushrooms.

6. Continue to wrap the meat in the strip of phyllo, folding on a diagonal (as if you were folding a flag) to form a triangle. Seal the edge of the phyllo with some melted butter. Repeat with the remaining strips until all the beef is used up.

7. Arrange the triangles on a baking sheet and bake in the preheated oven for about 10 minutes or until the tops puff up and are golden.

Note: If you are really out to impress someone, search out fresh truffles and mortgage your future to buy a few. Shave them into slivers over the beef before you fold the phyllo over it.

Shredded Pork Filling

8 ounces pork tenderloin, cut into thin,
1-inch-long slices
1 clove garlic, finely chopped
2 teaspoons soy sauce
2 to 3 pitted prunes, finely sliced

1. Spray skillet with vegetable spray and sauté the pork, if desired, until brown.

2. Combine the pork with the rest of the ingredients in a bowl and assemble and cook as for the Beef Wellington Filling (page 144).

Chicken Filling

2 skinless, boneless chicken breasts, lightly poached
Juice of 1 lemon
Salt and freshly ground black pepper to taste
Fresh rosemary sprigs
1 cup pistachio nuts, finely chopped

1. Slice the chicken into small, bite-size pieces and moisten with the lemon juice. Season with salt and pepper.

2. Assemble and cook as for the Beef Wellington Filling (page 144), placing a piece of chicken at the end of a phyllo strip, then placing a few rosemary sprigs and a sprinkle of pistachio nuts on top.

Fish Filling

8 ounces skinned and boned fillets of salmon, John Dory, monkfish, sole,
or pompano (or any other delicate, sweet-tasting fish)
1 bunch fresh watercress
Salt and freshly ground black pepper to taste
4 tablespoons ($\frac{1}{2}$ stick) unsalted butter

1. Cut the fillets into small, bite-size pieces. Sprinkle watercress leaves and salt and pepper over the fish. Assemble and cook as for the Beef Wellington Filling (page 144), placing a piece of fish at the end of a phyllo strip, then placing a pea-size dot of butter on top.

Dumplings and Empanadas

*D*umplings and empanadas make wonderful party food. I think of dumplings as more delicate than empanadas, simply because the wrappers are thin-textured and the dumpling fillings I most often use are more complex in their overall taste. Empanadas are more substantial because they are made with a crustlike dough and the filling is more ample. When I'm trying to decide which of the two to serve, I think about the other dishes I'm preparing and who will be eating them. If I'm going to have a large main course and most of the people attending are adults who will be mostly sitting or standing still (and thus able to handle the demands of accurate dipping and nibbling), I'll go with dumplings. Empanadas go well with casual fare, such as grilled food, and for this reason I make them a lot in the summer (made ahead, they're great for picnics). Children can run around with one empanada in their hands and another in their pocket; adults can plow through a whole plate while drinking a cold beer and then find room for a burger or a piece of poached fish.

I buy high-quality commercial dumpling skins and empanada wrappers. If you want to make your own, check out the recipe sources on page 49, where I have also explained how to fill dumplings and empanadas. Dumplings can be steamed in a steamer for about 10 minutes, boiled in lightly salted water for 5 minutes, or fried in very hot oil until golden and crispy.

Roast Pork Filling

2 tablespoons cornstarch
4 tablespoons water
1 tablespoon vegetable oil
1 cup chopped onion
8 ounces ground pork
2 tablespoons soy sauce
1 tablespoon sugar
Freshly ground black pepper to taste
¼ cup chopped scallions

1. In a small bowl, stir together the cornstarch and water and set aside. Heat the oil in a medium skillet. Add the onion and cook over medium heat for about a minute, just until translucent. Add the pork and cook until browned. Stir in the soy sauce, sugar, and pepper to taste. Stir in the cornstarch mixture and the scallions until mixed well with the meat. Set aside to cool before making dumplings.

MAKES ENOUGH FOR 12 FAT DUMPLINGS.

Curried Chicken Filling

1 skinless, boneless chicken breast, coarsely chopped
4 teaspoons cornstarch
2 tablespoons chicken stock
2 tablespoons vegetable oil
1 tablespoon dry sherry
½ cup chopped onion
1½ teaspoons curry powder
1 teaspoon sugar
3 tablespoons chopped scallions, white parts only

1. Combine the chicken with 1 teaspoon of the cornstarch in a medium bowl. Cover and set aside for 30 minutes. Stir together the stock and the remaining cornstarch. Set aside.

2. Heat 1 tablespoon of the oil in a medium skillet. Add the chicken and cook over medium-high heat, stirring constantly, until just cooked through, about 5 minutes. Add the sherry and mix to coat the chicken evenly. Remove the chicken to a bowl.

3. Heat the rest of the oil. Add the onion and cook over medium heat until just translucent. Add the curry powder and stir to coat the onion. Stir in the sugar and the chicken. Add the cornstarch-stock mixture, then the scallions. Cool to room temperature before making dumplings.

MAKES ENOUGH FOR 12 FAT DUMPLINGS.

Spicy Lamb Filling

2-inch piece fresh ginger, peeled
1 small onion
1 medium carrot
8 ounces ground lamb
1 large egg
1 tablespoon soy sauce
1 teaspoon curry powder
1 teaspoon sugar
1 teaspoon Chinese chili sauce
$\frac{1}{2}$ teaspoon salt
Vegetable oil, for frying

1. Finely chop the ginger in the bowl of a food processor fitted with the metal blade. With the motor running, drop the onion and carrot through the feed tube and process until finely chopped. Transfer to a bowl. Add the lamb to the bowl and add the remaining ingredients except for the oil. Mix well. Assemble the dumplings. Heat the oil and fry the dumplings until golden and crisp.

MAKES ENOUGH FOR 12 FAT DUMPLINGS.

Scallop Filling

¹/₄ cup loosely packed fresh cilantro leaves
1-inch piece fresh ginger, peeled
1 medium carrot
4 dried black mushrooms, stems removed and
soaked in hot water until soft
3 medium scallions, trimmed and cut into long pieces
8 ounces sea scallops
1 tablespoon dry sherry
1 tablespoon oyster sauce
1 teaspoon freshly grated lemon zest
Freshly ground black pepper to taste
1 tablespoon toasted sesame seeds, for garnish

1. In the bowl of a food processor fitted with the metal blade, finely chop the cilantro leaves. Drop the ginger through the feed tube and process until finely chopped. Add the carrot through the feed tube and pulse about 10 times. Transfer to a medium bowl.

2. Process the mushrooms with the scallions until finely chopped. Add to the bowl with the carrot. Process the scallops and add them to the bowl. Stir in the sherry, oyster sauce, lemon zest, and pepper to taste and mix thoroughly. Sprinkle with sesame seeds after the dumplings are cooked.

MAKES ENOUGH FOR 12 FAT DUMPLINGS.

Traditional Empanada Filling

This is a traditional recipe from South America. I've used all of the dumpling filling recipes in this book in empanadas as well.

2 tablespoons vegetable oil
2 tablespoons chopped onion
2 cloves garlic, finely chopped
16 ounces sirloin hamburger
10 Mediterranean black olives, pitted and finely chopped
1/4 cup loosely packed fresh cilantro leaves, chopped
2 tablespoons tomato paste
1/2 teaspoon ground cumin
1/4 teaspoon ground red pepper
1/4 teaspoon ground turmeric
1 large egg, lightly beaten, for brushing

1. Preheat the oven to 400°F.

2. Heat the oil in a skillet. Add the onion and garlic and sauté over medium heat until the onion is translucent. Add the meat and cook thoroughly, stirring occasionally. Add the remaining ingredients except for the egg and stir well to mix. If the mixture looks dry, add water, 1 tablespoon at a time, until you have a little bit of a sauce surrounding the meat (but it should not be too liquidy). Take a taste and season to your liking, adding salt and pepper, if desired.

3. Fill the empanadas following the instructions on page 50. Place the filled empanadas on a lightly greased baking sheet, brush the tops with the egg, and bake for about 15 minutes or until lightly golden. Cool slightly but serve warm.

MAKES ENOUGH FOR 48 (4-INCH-WIDE) EMPANADAS.

Dips

I have served all of these dips with all three styles of hors d'oeuvres, though I think phyllo and empanadas are better off with the simpler dips, such as the yogurt or the horseradish sauce. For dumplings, where the wrapper adds very little to the overall flavor of the filling, I have often served several different dips at once to provide variety and contrast. Each of these recipes yields enough dip for at least 24 small hors d'oeuvres.

Yogurt Dip: This dip is especially good with spicy food. Combine 1 cup plain yogurt with about ¼ cup finely chopped fresh mint.

Horseradish Sauce: I like to serve this one with fish and beef.

> *½ cup heavy cream, chilled*
> *2 tablespoons white wine vinegar*
> *1½ tablespoons strong horseradish*
> *Salt and pepper to taste*

1. Whip the cream until soft peaks form. Whisk in the vinegar, 1 tablespoon at a time. Whisk in the horseradish and salt and pepper to taste.

Aioli Sauce: This is especially good with vegetables, chicken, and fish.

> *1 whole garlic bulb, cloves separated and peeled*
> *2 large egg yolks*
> *Juice of 1 lemon*
> *1 teaspoon Dijon mustard*
> *Salt and freshly ground black pepper to taste*
> *1½ cups olive oil*

1. In the bowl of a food processor fitted with the metal blade, chop the garlic cloves, pulsing 2 or 3 times. Stop the motor and add the egg yolks, lemon juice, mustard, and salt and pepper. Process until smooth. With the motor running, add the olive oil through the feed tube. Process until you have a thick paste.

Mustard-Dill Dip: This goes well with fish.

$^{1}/_{2}$ cup Dijon mustard
$^{1}/_{2}$ cup plain yogurt
$^{1}/_{2}$ cup chopped fresh dill

1. Mix all of the ingredients together.

Plum-Mustard Dip: I like to serve this dip with pork.

1 tablespoon dry mustard
2 tablespoons hot water
$^{1}/_{2}$ cup plum sauce
3 tablespoons rice vinegar
1 tablespoon sesame oil
1 tablespoon soy sauce
1 tablespoon sugar

1. Stir the mustard and water together, then add the remaining ingredients and blend until smooth.

Scallion-Cilantro Dip: This recipe and the next two can be served with just about anything.

3 tablespoons fresh cilantro leaves
1-inch piece fresh ginger, peeled
1 large scallion, diced
1 tablespoon soy sauce
1 tablespoon sesame oil
2 teaspoons red wine vinegar
1 teaspoon chili oil
$^{1}/_{2}$ teaspoon sugar

1. In the bowl of a food processor fitted with the metal blade, mince the cilantro, ginger, and scallion. Add the remaining ingredients and pulse 2 or 3 times to mix.

Chinese Vinaigrette

1 clove garlic
1-inch piece fresh ginger, peeled
2 medium scallions, white part only, cut into 1-inch pieces
$^1/_4$ cup loosely packed fresh cilantro leaves
1 tablespoon soy sauce
1 tablespoon dry sherry
1 tablespoon sesame oil
1 tablespoon red wine vinegar
1 teaspoon hoisin sauce
$^1/_2$ to 1 teaspoon Chinese chili paste
$^1/_2$ teaspoon sugar

1. Place all of the ingredients in the bowl of a food processor fitted with the metal blade and blend until the garlic, ginger, scallion, and cilantro are finely chopped.

Simple Dipping Sauce

$^1/_2$ cup rice vinegar
1 tablespoon finely shredded fresh ginger
2 teaspoons chili sauce

1. Mix all of the ingredients together.

What's for Dinner?

*Why does it take so much trouble to
keep your stomach full and quiet?*

—SHIRLEY ANN GRAU, *THE KEEPERS OF THE HOUSE*

Some of the worst things I've eaten—and indeed cooked—have been savory pies. Most of them *looked* so delicious, their crust polished with a glaze of egg whites and perhaps embellished with shapes made from leftover dough. But when they were broken into—literally, sometimes having to be smashed to bits—what a mess awaited inside.

Savory pies can be time-consuming and tricky to construct, their pastry often the victim of all the major pitfalls of pie-making. If crusts have trouble surrounding simple fruit fillings, think of the hazards faced by those that must encase thick sauces, weeping vegetables, or juicy chunks of meat.

And yet, when I was reviewing restaurants back in the eighties (almost every chef in New York was rediscovering the essence of American cooking—the period of buffalo steaks, elk fillets, and rattlesnake shish kebab), I had a chicken pie the memory of which I have yet to forget.

My boss was reviewing a restaurant and invited a few other reviewers along for the meal. We were there just to share a bit of our meals with him and help him figure out how they were made. While I looked over the menu, my boss helped everyone select their meal. By the time he got to me, the only dish left was the chicken pie. Suffice it to say, it was not my first choice. I couldn't stand even the thought of dinner pies. I'd never succeeded at my attempts to make one, and I still couldn't shake the memory of the frozen chicken potpies my mother left for my brother and me on Saturday nights when she and my dad went out on their weekly date. (So tired were we of those potpies that my brother and I started cooking for ourselves on those nights, taking recipes from an old paperback copy of *Mastering the Art of French Cooking* that my worldly Aunt Margie left behind after one of her visits!) When the chicken pie was selected for me in that fancy restaurant, I felt like I was ten again, and I believe I even got a little cranky about it. I could choose my own dessert, my boss cajoled.

I wasn't taken in when the pie came, presented in a plain white crock, its upper crust decorated with a crowing chicken in pastry bas-relief. I brought my fork down hard upon its beak, anticipating having to break it hard, but the tines sank right in, the layers of pastry flaking away to reveal a golden broth blushing with saffron, and sweet chicken meat sharpened by finely chopped broccoli rabe. I knew right away that this was not something I wanted to share, even with my good-natured boss. However, in a sweetly menacing tone that seemed to involve my next paycheck, he insisted, and I reluctantly passed him a larger portion than I really wanted him to have.

I went home that night wondering why I couldn't make a pie as delicious as that one and I have come back to the same question often since then. It is all too rare to find something as wholesome and delicious as that pie. It also, and I say this cautiously, started me wondering about our national character. Although we have grown up to be a nation of pie eaters, so much in love with

Mincemeat

I have come to think of mincemeat pie as a fine illustration for America's melting pot. It was first brought to our shores by the earliest English settlers and was long considered an essential part of the pantry's store. The original recipe combines a meat, usually boiled beef (but sometimes game), suet, and a quantity of tart apples, all finely chopped together and added to preserved, dried (or pickled) pieces of fruit, such as cherries, lemons, currants, or raisins, plus sugar and boiled cider. All of this was spiced with nutmeg, cinnamon, mace, cloves, and salt and simmered in broth until quite tender, then the mincemeat destined for quick use was packed into a stoneware crock and a film of brandy was floated on top; the rest was locked into canning jars. With all the chopping and stirring involved, mincemeat was an exhausting project, one of the chores often shared by the women in a community after the autumn slaughter.

Almost as soon as mincemeat reached the colonies, however, the basic recipe began to change. Different nationalities influenced the recipes that evolved. Scottish and Irish settlers used fewer spices. A recipe from a German native substituted pork and also slipped in some cabbage. A Swedish farmwife in Minnesota added walnuts and anise. An 1886 cookbook was influenced, as the flyleaf says, in the "French manner" and suggested adding more sugar (up to a pound more!) and substituting butter for suet.

As Harriet Beecher Stowe noted in her novel *Old Town Folks*, "The pie is an English institution which, planted on American soil, forthwith ran rampant and burst forth into an untold variety of genera and species. Not merely the old traditional mince pie, but a thousand strictly American seedlings from that main stock, evinced the power of American housewives to adapt old institutions to new uses."

pies that we have embraced one of them as a national treasure, it is mostly dessert pies that we have taken to heart. There was a time when dinner pies were a part of almost every household's weekly menu. They made short work of leftovers from the Sunday roast and were often relied upon to stretch meager provisions to feed as many mouths as possible. Now, however, dinner pies are rarely made on a regular basis because even the simplest version requires many steps. If they are thought of at all, savory pies are reserved for special occasions.

It was a special occasion when I made my first savory pie—my first Christmas Eve as a wife—and I wanted to make something both traditional and unusual for my husband. It was important to me to present him with an imposing holiday spread. I envisioned a great, Dickens-inspired, groaning board of roasted meats and steamed puddings, the spicy perfume of mulled wine wafting through the apartment. In the weeks leading up to the holidays, I poured over cookbooks and the latest issues of food magazines until I came up with what I thought of as the perfect centerpiece for the meal: a steak-and-kidney pie. Although I had never eaten one, this dish recommended itself to me because it was one Chris remembered fondly from his time at the University of York and, I discovered, one that would amply—and cheaply—feed the horde Chris eventually invited as the holiday drew near. He would be working until 4 P.M. on Christmas Eve and, after a holiday toast at the office, he and most of the paper's single reporters would make their way to our place for dinner.

I started preparations early. It was snowing outside and our attic apartment was freezing, the windowpanes laced from the inside out with frost. The recipe I chose to guide me was from a fairly old British cookbook that gave scant instructions. I used *Joy of Cooking* as a backup. All afternoon I diced and sautéed, made a potent wine sauce from the juices in the skillet, and then rolled out the crust. The instructions called for a very strong crust and I used the recipe Betty gave me. I rolled it out as even and thin as could be, then laid it gently in a clay casserole. I spooned the steak and kidney inside, then poured the juices over everything. I laid another sheet of pastry over the top, made pretty decorations out of the extra dough and pressed them around the edges to seal the pie, then popped it in the oven. I set the table, put "Merry Christmas, Baby" on the stereo, and, ready for my husband and guests to arrive, poured myself a holiday glass of wine.

Twenty minutes later the apartment was thick with smoke, the pungent stench of baking kidney overwhelming the weaker scent of the freshly cut Christmas tree. I peeked inside the oven and saw that the juices were bubbling over the sides of the dish and the top crust was sinking into the filling. The only solution I could think of was to put another layer of dough over the submerged top, but when I went to place the pastry over the hot filling, the steam from the meat quickly melted the dough even before I got it across the dish.

Well, hell, I said to myself. The downstairs door opened and I heard the laughter and heavy tread of our guests as they stomped off the snow and began to climb the stairs. I shoved the mess back into the oven right before they opened the door. As the dinner hour approached, I slipped away to the kitchen, quickly boiled up some noodles, and spooned the beef and the sauce over them (the kidneys went to our appreciative cats). The mulled wine and the large glass bowl filled with trifle got me through the rest of the evening.

It took me five years to forget that experience and to even consider again making a savory pie. But I did want to re-create the chicken pie I had at that restaurant and so I eventually went to work. Easily the first half dozen varieties I made were disastrous failures, the kinds of flops I didn't have the courage to present even to my closest friends. I was grateful for our two big dogs and the pile of cats living with us, though I realized all that soggy dough couldn't be good for them. My continuing problem was the crust. It either came out too tough to eat or too weak to hold the filling. A dinner pie requires a very different kind of pastry than a dessert pie and it took me a while to settle on a pâte brisée. This crust will not wilt nor grow soggy even with the juiciest of fillings and, brushed with a light film of egg whites, it comes out of the oven golden and shiny and ready to break easily into fine buttery layers. There is only one problem—pâte brisée has to be made at least two hours ahead, which requires that I plan my life a little more than usual. This resting period breaks up any rubbery quality that may have crept in while working the dough into a smooth ball. The longer it rests, the better the crust is—flakier and more tender. For that reason alone, I strongly suggest that beginners make the crust one day and the filling for the pie the next day, especially if the pie is meant to impress someone.

Let me also warn beginners not to roll the savory crust pastry too thin. One of my problems with a top crust was rolling out a beautifully thin sheet of pastry only to see it melt into the filling when I draped it over a wide casserole dish. Remember that, except in a few recipes, the pastry won't be sitting on top of a firm, cold filling. It must have the thickness and strength to span the dish opening without absorbing a lot of liquid from the filling. To further avoid losing your crust before it even gets to the oven, choose a deep baking dish or pie pan with a small diameter.

Other savory crust options are biscuit dough or mashed potatoes. Because biscuit dough does not stand up to the steam of a hot filling, it should be used only as a top crust and, even then, layered over the pie only in the final cooking stages (see page 45 for the recipe and further instructions). Mashed potatoes are more resilient. You can either spread a layer of potatoes into a casserole or pie plate and then fill the center with a meat or vegetable filling or, as in shepherd's pie, spoon them over the filling as you would for meringue, making small peaks and crags with the back of a spoon for a pretty effect.

Sometimes I mash a lot of extra potatoes and make them into individual shells, then freeze them for future use with any leftovers I have on hand. They make a wonderful quick meal and have the appeal of looking like I did a whole lot of special work. Directions on how to make the shells are given on page 47.

AMONG THE RECIPES in this chapter, I have included a few strictly for their historical interest. I have, for instance, never cooked a squirrel pie, and the closest I've come to venison is when our neighbor across the street drove down our block with a deer tied to his front bumper. After he did one of the most amazing parallel-parking jobs I've ever seen (taking into consideration overhanging hooves), he proceeded to butcher the poor thing right out in front of his apartment building. The stream of drawn blood that ran in the gutter drew a car full of cops who thought a massacre was taking place. The faces of even our hardest local delinquents blanched as the man continued to dress the deer, even as one cop wrote him out a summons for violating a city ordinance.

In any case, I have included these recipes only after receiving a strong promise from the people who gave them to me—and whose taste I trust—that they are, indeed, delicious. I present them in the spirit of our ancestors, who once filled their new homes in this country with the fragrance of slow-baking savory pies.

Chicken Potpie

*D*espite my mom's reliance on frozen dinners, occasionally she would make chicken pies from scratch. They were a favorite of my dad's, and when he came home late at night after raising hell at a community meeting, she would heat him up a slice and serve it to him with a cold beer. This is the recipe my mom says she used most often, sometimes substituting spinach for the broccoli because my dad liked it better.

Single 9-inch Pâte Brisée crust (page 42), unbaked

Filling:
1 cup water
1 cup white wine
3 whole chicken breasts or 6 thighs, skinless
3 tablespoons unsalted butter
3 tablespoons all-purpose flour
1 cup milk
1 small head fresh broccoli, spears only
(or about $^1/_2$ pound fresh spinach, well washed and leaves
removed from stems and shredded)
$^1/_4$ cup chopped scallions
$^1/_4$ cup grated Parmesan cheese
Paprika to taste
Freshly ground black pepper to taste
1 large egg yolk, lightly beaten, for brushing

1. Prepare the pâte brisée.

2. Preheat the oven to 425° F.

3. In a large pot set over medium heat, bring the water and wine to a boil. Reduce to a simmer, add the chicken pieces, and lightly poach in the liquid for about 10 minutes or until the meat is just cooked. Remove the chicken and reduce the cooking liquid to 1 cup. Reserve. Remove the chicken meat from the bones and cut into bite-size pieces.

4. In a large saucepan over medium heat, melt the butter. Add the flour, stirring to form a paste. Slowly stir in the reserved broth and the milk until smooth, then bring the liquid just to the boiling point and simmer for 5 minutes or until thickened.

5. Stir the broccoli spears (or spinach), scallions, reserved chicken meat, and cheese into the sauce. Sprinkle with paprika and pepper to taste.

6. Turn the chicken mixture into a buttered 8-cup casserole dish. Roll out the pâte brisée and arrange it carefully over the top of the casserole. Press the pastry over the edges of the dish and seal over the edges. Slash a few vents across the top of the crust to allow steam to escape and brush with a little beaten egg yolk.

7. Bake in the center of the oven for 35 minutes or until the crust is golden.

SERVES AT LEAST 6, WITH LEFTOVERS
FOR MIDNIGHT SNACKING.

Turkey, Spinach, and Ricotta Torte

*T*his recipe came to me from Cuisinart's *The Pleasures of Cooking* magazine, part of an article about what to do with leftover Thanksgiving turkey. It is one of the most elegant of leftover solutions, though I like it so much that I sometimes buy turkey breasts just for this pie. If you do use fresh breasts, poach the meat before you begin and use the cooking liquid in place of the stock in the recipe. The torte requires a slew of pots and pans, which is intimidating, but the actual working of the recipe is fairly simple. It is a very filling dish that requires nothing more than a green salad, a good bottle of wine, and a warm dessert to accompany it.

Double 9-inch Pâte Brisée crust (page 42), unbaked

Filling:
½ cup loosely packed fresh parsley leaves
2 ounces Parmesan cheese
1 clove garlic
1 medium onion, quartered
1 pound spinach leaves (fresh or frozen), stems removed
¼ cup chicken stock
About 2 cups cooked turkey meat, cut into bite-size pieces
Salt and freshly ground black pepper to taste
2 tablespoons unsalted butter
4 ounces slab bacon, diced
2 large eggs
1½ cups ricotta cheese
¼ cup heavy cream
1 large egg lightly beaten with 1 tablespoon water, for brushing

1. Prepare the pâte brisée.

2. Place a baking sheet on a rack in the center of the oven to catch spills. Preheat the oven to 425° F. Lightly oil a deep 9-inch or smaller tart pan with a removable bottom.

3. On a lightly floured surface, roll out half of the dough. Fold the pastry over the rolling pin and drape over the prepared pan. Gently press the dough into the bottom and against the sides of the pan. If the dough tears, patch with a little bit of extra dough and a drop of water. Place the tart pan in the refrigerator while you make the filling.

4. In the bowl of a food processor fitted with the metal blade, finely chop the parsley and Parmesan cheese. Transfer to a large bowl and set aside.

5. Drop the garlic through the feed tube with the motor running and process until finely chopped. Scrape down the work bowl. Add the onion and finely chop. Remove to a small bowl and set aside.

6. In a large covered saucepan over medium-low heat, bring $\frac{1}{4}$ cup water to a boil. Add the spinach and cook until just wilted. Drain and squeeze dry. Coarsely chop in the food processor and reserve.

7. Warm the stock in a small saucepan. Stir in the turkey meat and remove from the heat. Season with salt and pepper to taste.

8. Melt 1 tablespoon of the butter in a large skillet. Add the bacon and cook over medium heat until lightly browned. Remove the bacon with a slotted spoon and drain on a paper towel. Add the bacon to the parsley-Parmesan mixture.

9. Discard all but 2 tablespoons of the fat from the skillet. Add the garlic-onion mixture and cook, stirring, until soft and lightly browned, about 5 minutes. Stir in the remaining butter and the cooked spinach. Cook, stirring, until heated through. Season to taste with salt and pepper, then add the parsley-Parmesan mixture.

10. Place the eggs, ricotta cheese, and cream in the food processor and process until blended. Add to the skillet and mix well. Fold in the turkey meat and pan juices. Adjust seasonings.

11. Spoon the filling into the prepared tart pan and smooth the top.

12. Roll out the remaining dough. Drape it over the rolling pin and center it over the filling. Trim the overhang of both crusts to 1 inch. Moisten the edges of the top and bottom crusts and gently press together, folding them over together to form a ridge along the top. Lightly brush the top with the egg wash.

13. Cut a circle about the size of a half-dollar out of the middle of the top crust. Bake on the baking sheet for 15 minutes. Reduce the heat to 350°F and continue baking for 1 more hour or until the top crust is nicely browned. Cover loosely with foil if the crust begins to brown too much.

14. Cool for 5 minutes before serving. Remove the sides of the tart pan and cut into wedges.

SERVES AT LEAST 6.

Double-Crust Chicken Pie

*T*his recipe and the two that follow came from my friend Alison's mother, who was born in Mississippi but ended up in Lubbock, Texas, a turn of events Alison said her mother never quite got used to. When Alison's mother served one of these dishes, all her children knew she was missing her childhood home. When I was first given these recipes, I made the mistake of thinking they were all very similar and when I said so to my friend, her pride in her Southern heritage emerged and she made some thinly veiled remark about Northerners being ignorant numskulls. Well, they do read as if they were similar, but they cook up entirely differently.

In the first recipe, the chicken is cooked on the bone for added flavor.

The second is rather light and good for a noonday meal, while the third is perfect for a cold winter's dinner.

Double recipe Biscuit Crust dough (page 45)

Filling:
2 broiler chickens (2½ pounds each), cut into serving pieces
Salt to taste
Paprika to taste
8 tablespoons (1 stick) unsalted butter (margarine can be substituted),
at room temperature
Freshly ground black pepper to taste
2 cups boiling water

1. Preheat the oven to 450°F.

2. Make the biscuit dough and divide into 4 equal portions.

3. Pat the chicken dry and sprinkle well with salt and paprika.

4. Roll out a portion of dough to a thickness of about ¼ inch. Cut into 1 × 2-inch strips and lay the strips over the bottom of a buttered 4-quart baking dish. Top with half the chicken pieces.

5. Dot the chicken pieces with some of the butter and sprinkle with pepper.

6. Roll out the second dough portion and cut as before, laying the strips over the chicken until covered. Place the rest of the chicken over this pastry layer, dot with butter, and sprinkle with pepper.

7. Roll out the third dough portion so that it is large enough to cover the top of the dish. Seal it around the edges. Cut a small hole in the center and pour just enough boiling water into it to barely float the crust.

8. Bake in the center of the oven for about 15 minutes or until brown. Remove from the oven and spread about 2 tablespoons softened butter over the top crust.

9. Roll out the remaining dough and place over the top of the crust, sealing the edges against the bottom crust.

10. Return to the center of the oven and bake for 10 minutes or until the second crust is lightly browned. Remove from the oven and spread the top crust with more softened butter.

11. Reduce the oven temperature to 325°F and bake for 45 minutes or until the chicken is tender. You can check if the chicken is tender by poking a skewer through the crust into a piece of meat. If it passes through easily, the chicken is done.

S ERVES 6 TO 8.

Chicken Spoon Bread Pie

Filling:
5 tablespoons chicken fat (butter or olive oil
can be substituted)
¼ cup chopped celery
2 tablespoons chopped onion
5 tablespoons all-purpose flour
2½ cups chicken stock
2 teaspoons chopped fresh parsley
2 teaspoons fresh thyme

Salt and freshly ground black pepper to taste
2½ cups cooked chicken, cut into bite-size pieces

Spoon bread:
2 cups boiling water
1 cup white cornmeal
2 tablespoons unsalted butter, at room temperature
1 cup milk
4 large eggs, well beaten
3 teaspoons baking powder
1 teaspoon salt

1. Preheat the oven to 400°F.

2. To make the filling, melt the fat in a medium saucepan. Add the celery and onion and cook over medium heat until just soft. Stir in the flour. Add the chicken stock and cook, stirring constantly, until the mixture boils and thickens slightly. Add the parsley, thyme, salt, and pepper. Stir in the chicken and heat through.

3. Pour the mixture into a 3-quart casserole and place in the oven to heat while you make the spoon bread.

4. To make the spoon bread, pour the boiling water over the cornmeal in a large bowl. With a wooden spoon, beat in the butter, milk, eggs, baking powder, and salt to form a smooth batter.

5. Pour over the chicken in the casserole and bake in the center of the oven for 40 to 45 minutes or until the top is brown. Serve at once.

SERVES 6 TO 8.

Country Chicken Pie

*T*he crust for this pie is almost like a bread. The bacon fat gives it a nice flavor, though it's probably not what your doctor would want you to eat all the time. Out of habit, I use this crust only for this recipe, but there's no reason in the world why you couldn't use it for other savory pies.

Crust:
¾ cup scalded milk
6 tablespoons sugar
5 tablespoons bacon fat
1 package active yeast
2 large eggs, lightly beaten
1 teaspoon salt
¼ teaspoon baking soda
3 cups sifted all-purpose flour

Filling:
2 tablespoons olive oil
2½ pounds chicken, boned and cut into bite-size pieces
1 cup chopped onion
1 (24-ounce) can whole tomatoes,
drained and chopped
½ cup dry red wine
¼ teaspoon dried thyme
¼ teaspoon dried rosemary
Salt and freshly ground black pepper to taste
1 large egg yolk, lightly beaten, for brushing

1. To make the crust, place the milk, 1 teaspoon of the sugar, and the bacon fat in a small saucepan over low heat. Cook until the fat is melted and the sugar is dissolved. Remove from the heat and add the yeast. Let the mixture stand until the surface bubbles. Pour the mixture into a large bowl and stir in the eggs, salt, baking soda, and the rest of the sugar. Add the flour, 1 cup at a time, to the mixture, beating until smooth after each addition. When all the flour is added, cover the dough with a cloth and put in a warm spot to rise until doubled in size, about 1 hour.

2. Turn the dough out onto a floured surface. Knead once or twice, then shape into 2 disks. Wrap 1 disk in plastic wrap and store in the refrigerator. Roll out the other disk to a thickness of about ¼ inch and gently lay it in a very deep pie pan or casserole dish.

3. To make the filling, heat the oil in a large skillet over medium heat. Add the chicken and onion and sauté until the chicken is slightly cooked and the onion is soft. Add the tomatoes, wine, herbs, salt, and pepper. Cook over medium heat until the juices have thickened and reduced by half, about 30 minutes. Remove from the heat and let cool.

4. Preheat the oven to 425°F.

5. Pour the cooled chicken mixture into the prepared crust. Roll out the top crust and place over the mixture, folding the edges of the bottom crust over the top crust to seal. Slash a few vents across the top of the crust to allow steam to escape and brush the surface with the egg yolk.

6. Cover the rim of the crust with aluminum foil. Place the pie in the center of the oven and bake for 15 minutes. Reduce the heat to 350°F and bake for 45 minutes more. Remove the foil and continue baking another 15 minutes or until the crust is golden brown.

SERVES 6 TO 8.

Cornish Pasties

*P*asties got my husband through a bleak student year in York, England, where he spent a lot of energy bemoaning the gray sky and the English girls who thought he was nuts. He says that Guinness and pasties were the only things besides his studies that gave him pleasure. This is my grandmother's recipe; she used to make pasties for her crew every Saturday night. (See page 62 for another kind of pasty.)

Crust:
⅔ cup lard, chilled
½ cup finely diced suet, chilled
3 cups sifted all-purpose flour, chilled
Approximately ½ cup iced water

Filling:
1 medium onion, finely diced
3 medium potatoes, peeled and diced
3 carrots, diced into small chunks
¾ pound sirloin beef, coarsely chopped
¼ pound pork loin, coarsely chopped
Salt and freshly ground black pepper to taste
Unsalted butter

1. To make the crust, cut the lard and suet into the sifted flour until well mixed. It should resemble coarse cornmeal.

2. Stir ¼ cup of the iced water into the flour with a fork. Continue to add water, a little at a time, just until the dough comes together. Cover with a damp cloth and let rest for an hour.

3. Preheat the oven to 425°F.

4. To make the filling, combine the vegetables and meats in a large bowl. Season with salt and pepper and moisten with a little less than ½ cup water. The filling should be just damp, not swimming in water.

5. Divide the dough into 4 equal parts. Roll the first quarter out onto a floured surface to an approximate circle with a diameter of at least 6 inches. Use a saucer as a pattern to trim the dough into a true circle.

6. Mound one-fourth of the filling over half of the circle. Dot with butter. Pull the other half of the circle over the filling and seal the edges together by pulling the bottom edge over the top edge and pressing down. It should look like a fat crescent moon.

7. Repeat with the 3 remaining pieces of dough and the filling until you have 4 large pasties.

8. Place the pasties on a greased baking sheet and bake in the center of the oven for 10 minutes. Reduce the heat to 375°F and continue baking another 50 minutes or until a fork presses easily through the crust and into the potato pieces.

SERVES 4.

Scottish Bridies

This is another savory served in pubs in England and Scotland. If I know it's going to be a hectic week between work, school, and sport practices, I'll make a couple of batches and freeze them. Then when my kids are flying off to after-school activities, or one of us comes home late, I'll pop a few bridies in the microwave. These pastries are also delicious stuffed with chopped vegetables, such as cauliflower, potatoes, and winter squash.

Dough for a double 9-inch Butter and Lard Crust
(page 25), unbaked

Filling:
1 pound boneless beef chuck, well trimmed and
cut into 1-inch pieces
2 ounces beef suet, cut into 1-inch pieces
1 medium onion
$1/2$ teaspoon salt
$1/2$ teaspoon freshly ground black pepper
$1/4$ teaspoon dried thyme

1. Prepare the dough, roll it into a disk, and refrigerate while you make the filling.

2. Preheat the oven to 400°F.

3. In a food processor fitted with the metal blade, coarsely chop the meat and suet. Remove to a large bowl. Chop the onion and add to the meat mixture. Season with the salt, pepper, and thyme.

4. Divide the dough into 4 pieces. Roll each into an 8-inch circle. Spoon some filling onto 1 side of each circle of dough, leaving a $1/2$-inch border. Fold the dough over the filling and press the edges to seal. Make a small hole (about the size of a dime) in the center of each pastry and place on a baking sheet lined with parchment.

5. Bake in the center of the oven for 20 minutes. Reduce the heat to 350°F and bake about 35 minutes more or until the crust is golden brown.

SERVES 4.

Scottish Pies

The preparation for these pies spans a full twenty-four hours, so plan accordingly. When my children were younger, they used to love helping me shape the dough. It was like Play-Doh to them and the anticipation of seeing how the shapes held their form the next day seemed to intrigue them. Now they just want to eat the finished pies, so I don't tell them when I'm making them, and they're wonderfully surprised when I pull them out of the oven.

Crust:
¼ to ⅓ pound beef suet
2 tablespoons unsalted butter
2 teaspoons salt
7 tablespoons iced water
1 cup sifted cake flour
3 cups sifted all-purpose flour

Filling:
1 cup soft bread crumbs
1 teaspoon salt
Freshly ground black pepper to taste
Water
⅔ tablespoon chopped onion
1 pound ground mutton

1. In a medium saucepan over low heat, melt enough suet to measure 7 tablespoons. Add the butter and stir until it is melted.

2. Dissolve the salt in the water and set aside.

3. Pour the fat into a mixing bowl and add the 2 flours. Mix together until the mixture looks crumbly.

4. Make a well in the center of the flour and pour in the salt water. Combine well to form a dough and divide into 2 balls of slightly unequal size.

5. Roll out the larger ball of dough on a floured surface. Drape the sheet of dough over the underside of a 12-cup cupcake tin that you've sprayed lightly with nonstick cooking spray. Gently press the dough over the cups to mold into cup shapes, then set aside.

6. Roll out the remaining dough and cut out circles that are slightly larger than the mouths of the cupcake tin. Cut a small (dime-size) hole in the center of each circle. Place the circles on an ungreased baking sheet and put both the cupcake tin and the baking sheet in a cool, dry place for 24 hours to set the dough in shape.

7. Preheat the oven to 400°F.

8. To make the filling, combine the bread crumbs, salt, pepper, and enough water to moisten in a medium bowl. Add the onion and ground meat and mix thoroughly.

9. Carefully turn the cupcake tin over on an ungreased baking sheet and remove the tin. The sheet of pastry should retain the shape of the tin so that you have, in effect, a sheet of pastry cups.

10. Carefully fill each shell three-fourths of the way to the top with the filling. Place a circle top over each of the filled cups. Gently but firmly seal the edges of the tops around each cup.

11. Bake in the center of the oven for 30 minutes or until the dough is golden brown. The cups will collapse a bit as they cook and resemble large raviolis. To serve, cut the crust between the cups with a sharp knife and serve on a plate or a napkin.

MAKES 12 SMALL PIES. EACH PIE WILL SERVE 1 CHILD. MEN AND HUNGRY WOMEN WILL WANT 2.

Hearty Beef Pie

My brother, Joe, tells me he perfected this recipe when he was getting his master's degree and living in a basement apartment in Astoria, Queens, on about four hundred dollars a month. Two hundred dollars went to rent, the rest went to transportation and whatever other expenses he had. Very little was left over for food. He counted on coming to our apartment for at least one meal a week, and he always came out with me when I was reviewing a restaurant. Joe would also make this pie—usually on Sunday nights—and the leftovers got him through to the end of the week.

Single 9-inch Pâte Brisée crust (page 42), unbaked

Filling:
4 slices bacon, cut into 1-inch pieces
3 pounds beef cubes
¾ teaspoon salt
Freshly ground black pepper to taste
1 large onion, diced
4 medium carrots, diced
3 stalks celery, diced
½ pound mushrooms, sliced
1½ cups beef stock, fortified with
¼ cup full-bodied red wine
3 tablespoons all-purpose flour
1 (12-ounce) bottle stout
1 tablespoon Worcestershire sauce
1 teaspoon dried thyme

1. Preheat the oven to 350° F.

2. Cook the bacon in a large skillet over medium-high heat until crisp. Drain, reserving the fat.

3. Season the beef with salt and pepper, then brown the meat in the bacon fat. Remove the pieces with a slotted spoon to an 8-cup or larger baking dish. Sprinkle the bacon on top.

4. Sauté the onion, carrots, celery, and mushrooms in the remaining bacon fat until soft.

5. In a small bowl, whisk together $\frac{1}{2}$ cup of the stock with the flour. Stir the paste into the vegetables in the skillet, then add the remaining stock, stout, Worcestershire sauce, and thyme. Bring to a boil. Pour over the meat. Cover tightly and bake in the center of the oven for $1\frac{1}{2}$ hours.

6. While the filling is baking, prepare the dough for the crust and roll out to a thickness of no less than $\frac{1}{4}$ inch. When ready, take the baking dish out of the oven, remove the lid, and arrange the dough over the beef. Fold the edges under the lip of the dish to seal. Return to the oven and bake for 25 minutes more or until the crust is golden.

SERVES 6 TO 8.

Pork Pie

*T*his is the kind of pie that used to await farmworkers when they came in from the fields at night. Mrs. Fraizer, whose family has farmed land in the Berkshires around Northampton, Massachusetts, since the Revolution, gave me this recipe the summer I stayed at an artist colony near her home. She and I met each other in the colony's big kitchen when she came to offer her vegetables to the staff cook. Stark vegetarian fare was all the writers and artists were fed, and I was making a bowl of chocolate mousse from the pure local cream to stave off my hunger. Mrs. Fraizer revealed herself to be a fellow chocolate addict and we got to talking about food, the history of the area, and her life with her husband and four sons. When my time was up at the colony, she slipped me this recipe with the following notation: "This is a good way of satisfying men enough that they leave you alone to think in the evening."

I have never used any crust other than the one Mrs. Fraizer gave me for this recipe. I think it complements the filling perfectly.

Crust:
2²/₃ cups sifted all-purpose flour, chilled
1 teaspoon salt
³/₄ cup pork fatback, salt rinsed off, rind trimmed, and chilled
Approximately ¹/₂ cup iced water

Gravy:
2 cups homemade or canned chicken stock
2 tablespoons cornstarch
¹/₂ cup water

Filling:
2 cups peeled and thinly sliced potatoes
¹/₂ chopped cup onion
1¹/₂ pounds lean pork, cut into bite-size pieces
1¹/₂ teaspoons salt
2 tablespoons minced fresh parsley
¹/₂ teaspoon dried marjoram
Freshly ground black pepper to taste

1. Combine the flour and salt in a medium bowl. Cut the fatback into the flour and blend quickly until the mixture resembles cornmeal. Make a well in the center and pour in just enough iced water to bring the flour mixture together into a ball. Turn out onto a floured surface and knead once, forming the dough into a ball. Cover with plastic wrap and chill for about an hour.

2. To make the gravy, bring the stock to a boil over medium heat. Stir the cornstarch into the water, then add it in a steady stream to the stock, stirring constantly until the sauce thickens and is clear. Remove from the heat and set aside.

3. Preheat the oven to 350°F.

4. Roll out half the pastry and line a deep 2-quart casserole dish with it.

5. Arrange the potato slices on the bottom of the pastry. Spread the onion over the potatoes, then top with the pork. Season with the salt, parsley, marjoram, and pepper to taste. Pour the gravy over the top.

6. Roll out the remaining pastry and drape over the meat. Trim the edges and fold them under. Slash a few vents across the top of the crust to allow steam to escape.

7. Bake in the center of the oven for about $1\frac{1}{2}$ hours or until the crust is a rich, tawny brown. If the edges begin to burn, cover them with a strip of aluminum foil.

SERVES ABOUT 6 HUNGRY PEOPLE.

Super Bowl Pork Pie

*T*his is another pie that comes with its own crust recipe. The tablespoon of vinegar in the crust gives an added jolt of taste to the pork filling. It makes a fairly big pie, at least eleven inches, which makes it good for Super Bowl parties and other large, casual get-togethers.

Crust:
4 cups sifted all-purpose flour, chilled
1 tablespoon sugar
2 teaspoons salt
1³⁄₄ cups vegetable shortening, chilled
1 large egg
¹⁄₂ cup iced water
1 tablespoon cider vinegar

Filling:
2 pounds pork loin, cut into bite-size pieces
4 Granny Smith apples, peeled, cored, and thinly sliced
1 medium sweet onion, thinly sliced
2 tablespoons sugar
2 teaspoons ground sage
Salt and freshly ground black pepper to taste
¹⁄₂ cup apple cider
1 tablespoon unsalted butter
1 large egg, beaten, for brushing

1. In a large bowl, combine the flour, sugar, salt, and shortening. Blend just until the mixture resembles crumbs.

2. In a small bowl, mix together the egg, water, and vinegar. Drizzle the liquid over the flour and mix thoroughly.

3. Shape the dough into a disk, wrap in plastic wrap, and freeze for 30 minutes or refrigerate overnight.

4. Preheat the oven to 350°F.

5. Roll out half the dough to a thickness of about $\frac{1}{4}$ inch and use it to line a very deep 11-inch pie pan (a clay pie pan is perfect).

6. Place half the pork on the bottom of the pastry. Cover with half the apples, onion, sugar, and sage, and sprinkle with salt and pepper to taste. Repeat layers until all the meat is used. Pour the cider over the filling and dot with butter.

7. Roll out the remaining dough and place on top of the pie, crimping the edges. Slash a few vents across the top of the crust to allow steam to escape. Brush the crust with the beaten egg.

8. Bake in the center of the oven for $1\frac{1}{2}$ hours or until the top is nicely browned and the juices bubble up in the center. Remove from the oven and let stand at least 15 minutes before cutting.

S E R V E S   A T   L E A S T   6.

Squirrel Potpie

*T*he friend who gave me this recipe has fond boyhood memories of hunting with his brother in the woods around Pittsfield, Massachusetts. Both his parents worked in the textile mills and money was scarce. In the winter, the boys would go out with their squirrel guns and come back with enough meat for a few dinners.

The squirrel hunter came to New York to study sculpture and in the lean years, he told me, there were a few times he was tempted by the local critters, though the specimens he saw in the park were not like the ones back home; instead, he substituted inexpensive goat meat from a Middle Eastern butcher.

This recipe is from his mother, who must be a very good cook if the look in her son's eyes when he talks about the dish is any indication. You can use either the Biscuit Crust recipe on page 45 or the following one that my friend's mother gave me with the recipe. It is a buttermilk biscuit dough and has a nice undertone of sourness to it.

Crust:
2 cups sifted all-purpose flour, chilled
2 teaspoons baking powder
1 teaspoon salt
1/2 teaspoon baking soda
4 tablespoons (1/2 stick) unsalted butter,
chilled and cut into 4 pieces
1 cup cold buttermilk

Filling:
3 gray or fox squirrels, skinned and dressed,
cut into bite-size pieces
½ cup plus 1 tablespoon all-purpose flour
4 tablespoons (½ stick) unsalted butter, at room temperature
4 cups homemade chicken stock
1 onion, chopped
1 teaspoon salt
Freshly ground black pepper to taste

1. In a large bowl, combine the flour, baking powder, salt, and baking soda. Cut in the butter and blend quickly until the flour looks like cornmeal. Make a well in the center and stir in the buttermilk just until blended. Do not overstir.

2. Turn the dough out onto a lightly floured surface, knead it gently, then let it rest under a damp cloth while you make the filling.

3. Dredge the meat in ½ cup of the flour. Melt 2 tablespoons of the butter in a large Dutch oven. Add the meat and sauté over medium-high heat until brown. Add the stock, onion, salt, and pepper. Bring to a simmer, cover the pot with a tight lid, and cook until the squirrel meat is tender, about 1 hour.

4. Roll the biscuit dough out to a thickness of about ¼ inch and cut into rounds with the top of a glass or a biscuit cutter.

5. When the meat is ready, remove the lid from the pot and lay the biscuit rounds over the meat. Cover again and bring to a boil for 15 minutes. Transfer the dumplings and meat to a heated platter and set in a warm place.

6. Knead the remaining 2 tablespoons butter into the remaining 1 tablespoon flour. Add to the liquid in the Dutch oven, stirring well until the liquid thickens. Cook for about 5 more minutes at low heat. Pour the gravy over the meat and dumplings.

SERVES 6 TO 8.

Venison Pie

*T*his recipe came from the wife of my father's best friend, who used to give my family mittens made from deerskin. Attached was a note that said, "This is a good dish to make when the best parts are gone and you have only rump meat left."

Dough for a single 9-inch Pâte Brisée crust (page 42), unbaked

Marinade:
¾ bottle (about 2⅔ cups) full-bodied red wine
¼ cup olive oil
½ cup loosely packed fresh flat-leaf parsley, stems removed
3 crushed cloves garlic
2 tablespoons honey
1 teaspoon fresh thyme (½ teaspoon dried)
1 teaspoon dried marjoram
Salt and freshly ground black pepper to taste

Filling:
1½ pounds venison, trimmed and cut
into bite-size pieces
3 tablespoons unsalted butter
1 medium onion, thinly sliced
6 large mushrooms, sliced
3 medium potatoes, peeled and grated
3 large carrots, peeled and grated
1 large egg, beaten, for brushing

1. Combine all of the marinade ingredients in a large bowl. Add the venison, stir to coat with the marinade, then cover the bowl with plastic wrap and let the meat marinate in the refrigerator for at least 24 hours and up to 3 days.

2. Prepare the dough for the crust and refrigerate while you make the filling.

3. Preheat the oven to 400°F.

4. Melt the butter in a large frying pan. Add the onion and sauté over medium heat until translucent. Add the marinade from the meat. Bring to a boil, then turn down to a simmer until it is reduced by half.

5. When the sauce is ready, add the meat and then the mushrooms, potatoes, and carrots. Remove from the heat.

6. Roll out the dough for the crust on a lightly floured surface to a thickness of about $\frac{1}{4}$ inch. Gently lay the dough in a $9 \times 13 \times 4$-inch-deep casserole dish, pressing it into the bottom and along the sides, leaving at least 6 inches of dough hanging over the edges.

7. Pour the filling over the pastry, using just enough of the gravy to cover the meat. Gather the ends of the pastry up over the filling to meet in the middle. Try not to stretch the dough; if all the ends don't meet up, the space they leave will act as a vent. Seal shut the ends that do meet by giving them a good twist. If you have to, cut 2 small slits on either side of the twisted dough to allow steam to escape. Brush the top of the pie with the beaten egg.

8. Bake in the center of the oven for about 1 hour or until a knife poked through one of the slits can easily pierce a piece of meat.

SERVES ABOUT 6 TO 8.

Shepherd's Pie

Shepherd's pie is a comfort food for me and I long for it whenever I feel overwhelmed. Much to my chagrin, however, my children don't like mashed potatoes. So when I feel I must make this pie (which Chris is happy to share with me), I send them out for pizza.

A mashed potato crust can cover most anything. I outlined how to make individual mashed potato crusts that can be used to hold a filling on page 47. Here I give directions for a mashed potato top crust.

Crust:
4 cups mashed potatoes
1 large egg
6 tablespoons milk
Salt and freshly ground black pepper to taste

Filling:
1½ tablespoons unsalted butter
1 large onion, chopped
2 cups cooked lamb, cut into small cubes (other leftover cooked meat
can be substituted or mixed in)
½ cup peas
4 to 8 tablespoons leftover gravy or a mixture of
equal parts Worcestershire sauce and water
¼ teaspoon dried thyme
Salt and freshly ground black pepper to taste

1. Preheat the oven to 350°F.

2. To make the crust, in a large bowl beat the mashed potatoes with the egg, milk, and salt and pepper to taste. Set aside.

3. Melt the butter in a large skillet. Add the onion and sauté over medium heat until soft. Add the meat and peas and cook over low heat until the peas are slightly cooked. Stir in 4 tablespoons of the gravy or liquid, adding more if needed to make a moist filling. Add the thyme and salt and pepper. Taste a little to check seasoning and add more if needed. Remove the skillet from the heat.

4. Butter a 9-inch pie pan, then spread half the mashed potatoes in an even layer on the bottom and up the sides. Spoon the filling on top of the potatoes, then spread the rest of the mashed potatoes over the filling, making peaks with the back of the spoon.

5. Bake in the center of the oven for 45 to 50 minutes or until the potatoes are lightly browned. Serve immediately.

S E R V E S   2   O N   A   B A D   D A Y ,   4   O N   R E G U L A R   D A Y S .

English Veal and Ham Pie

A very traditional English pie. Any other meat can be substituted for the veal.

Double 9-inch Pâte Brisée crust (page 42), unbaked

Filling:
2 tablespoons vegetable oil
2 tablespoons finely chopped onion
1 pound cooked veal, cubed
½ pound cooked ham, coarsely chopped
2 teaspoons fresh, chopped parsley
½ teaspoon dried rosemary
1½ teaspoons freshly grated lemon zest
Salt and freshly ground black pepper to taste
1 cup chicken stock
1½ tablespoons cornstarch
2 tablespoons port (optional)
2 large hard-boiled eggs, sliced

1. Prepare the pastry. Line a 9-inch pie pan with half of the pastry and set aside in the refrigerator, along with the unrolled half, while you make the filling.

2. Heat the oil in a small skillet. Add the onion and sauté over medium heat until golden.

3. Combine the veal with the ham in a large bowl. Add the cooked onion, parsley, rosemary, lemon zest, salt, and pepper. Stir well to mix.

4. Bring the stock to a boil in a medium saucepan. Add the cornstarch and stir to dissolve. Boil for a couple of minutes until the stock thickens. Taste and correct seasoning, then add the port (if using) and set aside.

5. Take the pie pan out of the refrigerator and arrange half the meat mixture on the bottom. Top with the sliced eggs, then cover with the rest of the meat. Pour in the gravy.

6. Roll out the remaining pastry on a floured surface and position over the meat. Trim the sides and seal the edges. Slash a few vents across the top of the crust to allow steam to escape. Chill the pie for at least 30 minutes.

7. Preheat the oven to 450°F.

8. Set the pie in the lower third of the oven and bake for 20 minutes. If the edges are getting too brown, cover them with aluminum foil. Reduce the heat to 350°F and move the pie to the center shelf. Bake for 30 to 35 minutes more or until the pastry is a nice golden brown. Cool slightly before serving.

SERVES 4 TO 6.

Italian Sausage and Spinach Pie

A good treat for teenagers—and a way to get them to eat their spinach without a lot of back talk.

Single recipe Pizza and Calzone Crust
(page 43), unbaked

Filling:
1 pound hot Italian sausage, casings removed
1 pound fresh spinach, washed and stems removed,
coarsely chopped
4 ounces shredded mozzarella cheese
Olive oil, for brushing

1. Prepare the dough for the crust.

2. Crumble the sausage into small pieces in a large bowl.

3. Place the sausage in a large skillet over medium heat and cook until well browned. Remove from the heat and drain well.

4. Add the spinach to the sausage meat in the skillet and cook until the spinach wilts, about 3 minutes. Remove the skillet from the heat and set aside.

5. Preheat the oven to 400°F.

6. On a floured surface, roll out the dough to an approximate rectangle, about 12 inches wide and 10 inches long.

7. Transfer to an oiled baking sheet that is slightly larger than the rolled-out dough. Spoon the sausage mixture over half the dough, leaving a $\frac{1}{2}$-inch border. Sprinkle the mozzarella cheese over the meat.

8. Fold the dough over the filling and firmly press the edges together, crimping the edges to seal the sides. Brush the top with olive oil. Slash vents down the length of the pie to allow steam to escape.

9. Bake in the lower third of the oven for 15 to 20 minutes or until well browned.

S E R V E S   4   T O   6.

Shrimp Tart

*T*his tart is perfect for a light supper or as an accompaniment to a thick soup. The recipe looks long and involved but it really isn't.

*Single 11-inch Savory Tart Crust (page 41),
partially baked*

Filling:
2 tablespoons olive oil
1 tablespoon unsalted butter
1 small onion, finely chopped
1 small carrot, finely chopped
1 pound medium shrimp, with heads off, shelled, and cleaned
1/2 teaspoon dried thyme
1 bay leaf, crumbled
Pinch of ground red pepper
1/2 cup dry white wine
2 1/4 cups heavy cream
3 large eggs
2 large egg yolks
1/2 tablespoon tomato paste

1. Prepare the crust.

2. Preheat the oven to 350°F.

3. Heat the oil and butter in a large skillet over medium heat until the butter is melted. Stir in the onion, carrot, shrimp, thyme, bay leaf, and ground red pepper and cook, stirring constantly, until the shrimp begin to turn slightly pink, about 3 minutes. Remove the shrimp and set aside.

4. Stir the wine into the skillet and continue cooking the onion-carrot mixture until the liquid is reduced to a glaze, about 5 minutes. Remove from the heat and set aside.

5. In a food processor fitted with the metal blade, coarsely chop the shrimp. With the motor running, pour ¼ cup of the cream through the feed tube. Process until smooth, stopping to scrape down the bowl. Press the purée through a fine sieve into a bowl until all of the shrimp liquid is released. Reserve the liquid. In a large bowl, stir the shrimp purée with the onion-carrot mixture. Set aside.

6. Return the shrimp liquid to the processor and add the remaining cream, the eggs, egg yolks, and tomato paste. Pulse once or twice to mix. Fold the mixture in with the puréed shrimp mixture and pour it into the tart shell.

7. Bake for 40 to 45 minutes or until a knife inserted in the middle of the tart comes out clean. Let the tart stand for 10 minutes before serving.

SERVES 4.

Clam, Potato, and Bacon Potpie

*T*his is especially good after an exhausting day at the beach. Serve with a good bottle of white wine.

Double 9-inch Pâte Brisée crust (page 42), unbaked

Filling:
6 slices bacon
2 tablespoons unsalted butter
1 medium onion, finely chopped
3 tablespoons all-purpose flour
1 cup heavy cream

1 cup milk
1 pint shucked clams, chopped coarsely, reserving ¼ cup liquid
¼ teaspoon Worcestershire sauce
3 boiling potatoes, peeled and cut into ½-inch cubes
¼ teaspoon dried thyme
2 tablespoons finely chopped fresh parsley
1 teaspoon fresh lemon juice
Salt and freshly ground black pepper to taste
1 large egg yolk mixed with 1 tablespoon water, for brushing

1. Prepare the pâte brisée.

2. Preheat the oven to 400°F.

3. In a large stockpot, cook the bacon over medium heat until crisp. Remove to a paper towel to drain. Crumble and set aside.

4. Pour off all but 2 tablespoons of the bacon fat from the stockpot. Add the butter to the stockpot and melt. Add the onion and sauté over medium heat until soft. Add the flour and cook the roux until it turns a light tan. Add the cream, milk, reserved clam juice, and Worcestershire sauce and cook until the mixture thickens, about 5 minutes.

5. Add the potatoes, clams, thyme, parsley, lemon juice, crumbled bacon, and salt and pepper. Stir to mix well. Remove from the heat.

6. Divide the pâte brisée into 2 pieces, one slightly larger than the other. On a lightly floured surface, roll out the larger piece to a thickness of ¼ inch. Fit the pastry into a 9-inch pie pan, then trim the edges, leaving about a 1-inch overhang.

7. Pour the filling over the pastry. Roll out the remaining dough to a thickness of about ⅛ inch and arrange over the filling. Crimp the edges decoratively.

8. Brush the top crust with the egg wash and bake in the lower third of the oven for 35 minutes or until the top crust is golden.

SERVES 6 TO 8.

Oyster Pie

I'm going to record this recipe exactly as it is given in Mary Hooker Cornelius's *The Young Housekeeper's Friend*, which was published in 1864:

> Make a nice paste and lay down into a deep dish, turn a teacup down in the centre. This will draw the liquor under it, and prevent it from boiling over; it also keeps the upper crust from falling in and becoming clammy. Lay in the oysters, add a little pepper, butter and flour; make a wide incision in the upper crust, so that when the pie is nearly done, you can pour in half a teacup of cream or milk. Secure the edges of the crust and bake it an hour. It should be put into the oven immediately, else the under crust will be clammy. Use but little of the liquor.

I actually followed this recipe and I still can't figure out what you do with the cup when you go to serve the pie, but it did prevent the top crust from falling into the filling! If you wish to have a go, here is my version.

Double 9-inch Pâte Brisée crust (page 42), unbaked

Filling:
2 1/2 cups freshly shucked oysters, well drained
2 tablespoons unsalted butter
2 tablespoons all-purpose flour
Freshly ground black pepper to taste
1/2 cup heavy cream

1. Prepare the pâte brisée.

2. Preheat the oven to 350°F.

3. Line a deep 9-inch pie pan with half of the pâte brisée. Place a demitasse cup or other small heat-proof cup upside down in the middle of the crust. Arrange the oysters around the cup. Dot the oysters with the butter and sprinkle with the flour. Season with pepper.

4. Roll out the remaining dough and lay it gently over the top of the pie. Crimp and seal the edges. At the top of the pie where the cup is, cut a hole slightly smaller than the bottom of the cup. Slash a few vents across the top of the crust to allow steam to escape.

5. Bake in the center of the oven for 45 minutes. Pour the cream through the vents (not the hole!) and return to the oven to bake for 15 minutes more or until the top crust is a nice golden brown.

6. To serve, cut wedge-shaped slices up to the cup and carefully remove each slice to a plate. Admittedly, the slices will look a little funny, but the crust will be perfect.

S E R V E S 4.

Smoked Salmon Tart

*I*usually serve this for lunch or for an early dinner, accompanied by a salad and lots of good bread.

Single 11-inch Savory Tart Crust (page 41), baked

Filling:
½ pound smoked salmon, flaked
Approximately 3 sprigs fresh dill, or to taste
2 tablespoons unsalted butter
1½ tablespoons all-purpose flour

¹/₂ cup heavy cream
¹/₄ cup fish stock
2 large egg yolks
Juice from 1 medium lemon
Freshly ground black pepper to taste

1. Prepare the tart crust.

2. Preheat the oven to 350°F.

3. Arrange the salmon flakes and dill over the bottom of the crust.

4. Melt the butter in a medium saucepan over medium heat. Add the flour, cream, and stock and stir until the mixture is smooth. Boil gently for 5 minutes, being careful not to let the mixture burn on the bottom. Let cool a little, then add the egg yolks and lemon juice.

5. Pour the sauce over the fish and dust with pepper.

6. Bake in the center of the oven for 10 to 15 minutes or until the sauce has browned a little. Serve warm.

SERVES 4 TO 6.

Eggplant-Tomato Tart

*T*his is great in the summer and is just as delicious cold as hot.

Single 11-inch Savory Tart Crust (page 41), partially baked

Filling:
3 to 4 Italian eggplants
$^1\!/_3$ cup olive oil
Salt and freshly ground black pepper to taste
3 medium fresh tomatoes
2 large eggs
1 large egg yolk
1$^1\!/_2$ cups light cream
$^1\!/_2$ cup fresh basil leaves, thinly cut and loosely packed
$^1\!/_2$ cup shredded Gruyère cheese

1. Prepare the tart crust.

2. Preheat the oven to 375°F.

3. Peel the skin from the eggplants and slice the flesh into thin rounds that are no more than $^1\!/_8$ inch thick. Spray a baking sheet with nonstick cooking spray, lay the eggplant on the sheet, and brush the slices with the olive oil. Season with salt and pepper. Bake in the center of the oven until the slices are brown and tender but not completely soft —about 10 minutes.

4. Skin the tomatoes and slice them into rounds about as thick as the eggplants. Remove the seeds from the rounds.

5. Beat the eggs and yolk together, then whisk in the cream. Add a pinch of salt, a few grinds of fresh pepper, and the basil.

6. Scatter the cheese over the bottom of the partially baked tart shell, then loosely layer the eggplant and tomato rounds over the cheese. Pour the custard over them.

7. Bake the tart for about 35 to 40 minutes or until the custard sets. Let cool a bit before serving.

SERVES 4 TO 6.

Cromwell's Squash Tart

O ne of my best friends is a confirmed vegetarian. I still love her and hang out with her whenever I can. I made this tart for Kathleen when she and her sweetheart came over for Christmas dinner one year. While everyone else was devouring a good roast beef, she very contentedly forked her way through the tart.

Single 11-inch Savory Tart Crust (page 41), partially baked

Filling:
2 leeks
2 tablespoons unsalted butter
Salt and freshly ground black pepper to taste
2 large eggs
1/3 cup heavy cream
1/2 cup milk

*1 large winter squash, steamed and pulp scooped out
to make 1½ cups
3 ounces goat cheese, crumbled
½ teaspoon dried thyme
1 teaspoon fresh parsley*

1. Prepare the tart crust.

2. Preheat the oven to 375°F.

3. Quarter the leeks and wash well, then slice thinly. Melt the butter in a medium skillet. Add the leeks and sauté until just tender. Season with a sprinkle of salt and pepper to taste.

4. Beat the eggs in a large bowl with the heavy cream and milk, then add the squash and mix well. Stir in the leeks, cheese, and herbs. Season with salt and pepper.

5. Pour the batter into the tart shell and bake in the center of the oven until the center of the tart is firm, about 45 to 50 minutes. Remove from the oven and let rest for 5 to 10 minutes.

SERVES 4 TO 6.

Oh My!
You Shouldn't Have

Love is the open sesame to every human soul.

—Elizabeth Cady Stanton

One of the best reasons to make a pie is to give it to someone else. What makes giving a homemade pie as a gift special resides in the pie's reputation for being both difficult and homey; it conjures up both an arduous task and the comfort of a loving hand. But more important, to my mind at least, is the fact that when you give a person a pie, it can be meant for— and consumed by— that person alone.

This is how a single person eats an entire pie. The pie is presented to the ravenous person (usually a man, but children and honest women will recognize this, too), who is holding a fork. One slice is decorously cut and duly eaten from a little plate. Now the pie is open. All the beautiful bounty inside is exposed, and if the pie is delicious, the fork comes up as if on its own and digs right in, tine by tine breaking through the crust, scooping up the mess right from the pan until the bottom has been reached, excavated, and cleared.

I learned this about pies when I lived down south, where pies are the currency of hospitality. I shared an apartment in Atlanta, Georgia, with a woman from Lubbock, Texas. One of her first acts of kindness toward me was to make me a pecan pie after a particularly bad drinking night. She claimed that pecan pie is a potent cure for hangovers, explaining how the crust and nut-meats soak up the excess alcohol, while the sugar gives the blood much-needed energy. Though I was skeptical, I was grateful that she cared. She brought the finished pie to my room straight from the oven and as I sat up in bed and cra-dled the pan on my lap, its warmth spread down my legs and the rich sugary scent broke across my dulled senses. It must have worked passably, because pecan pie became a staple in our diet, an antidote to the many Happy Hours we attended in order to stretch our meager food budget. We lived on free bar food—chicken wings, spareribs, and popcorn—diluted drinks, and cheap beer. The pie was sometimes a morning necessity.

That was a miserably selfish time for me, as the early twenties are for many people, and though I recognized my roommate's generosity, I didn't really think about it much. I was too involved in my own discord, trying to figure out what I was doing so far away from home, in a job I didn't like much and at which I wasn't doing very well. I was also alone; Chris was up north pursuing his career as a journalist and had let me know before I left for Atlanta that he would be too busy to keep in touch. For a time, though, the life I hobbled together seemed good enough. I remember trying hard to succeed at my job. At night, I joined friends afterward at parties and clubs, and danced with men I never gave a second thought to. And yet, as the months went by, I began to drift apart from everything—ditching business meetings and canceling dates —to write. But even though the short stories and the book I was writing were receiving praise and a bit of acceptance from publications, I was dissatisfied. I knew my writing lacked compassion and, like the life I was leading then, my stories were hollow, almost cold, steering me into dead ends.

Even when you're young you can't go on like this for long. By Thanksgiving, when my brother, Joe, came down to spend the holiday with me, I was sick of pecan pie. We left the city and traveled down country roads, following the route of Sherman's march to the sea, and as I got farther and farther away from Atlanta, talking deeper and deeper to a person I loved, I began to realize what I wanted to do. Along the road there were truck stops and diners that advertised all-you-can-eat buffets and Joe, who considers it his solemn duty to do a thorough study of a region's cooking style, would pull in to compare the hush puppies or dirty rice we had in Decatur with the ones in Athens. In a restaurant near Andersonville, as Joe finished off a pile of fried catfish, I swallowed my pride and called Chris from a pay phone. I asked him how he was, and he said he missed me. We talked a few minutes more, and when I got back into my seat there was a slice of sweet potato pie with brown-sugar glaze waiting for me.

Joe told me it was on the house and pointed the end of his fork toward the waitress. "She said you looked like you needed it." I surely did and dug right in. When we got back to Atlanta, I quit my job and begged for a position on a project I had long admired, then I got rid of my dancing partners and booked a Christmas flight to Ohio to meet Chris.

When I returned to Atlanta in January, I went to work in a neighborhood called Mechanicsville. The neighborhood lay hard up against the expressway circling downtown Atlanta, south of the hill on which the government buildings rose and east of the great stadium that was built for the baseball team. A wide boulevard, down which most of the city's residents sped, cut it in half. On one side, Mechanicsville looked very much like any other poor, inner-city neighborhood. There were rows of housing projects beside desolate and underpopulated shopping centers, the modern architecture already pockmarked, nearly useless, and scarred with graffiti. The opposite side of the boulevard, however, was another world. Here, down small streets shaded by big oaks and sycamores, former slaves from the nearby plantations came to build homes after the Civil War. Most of the houses had remained in the hands of the original builders' descendants, added on to and embellished as the years passed and need arose. Because of the fire that destroyed antebellum Atlanta, these are some of the oldest buildings in the city. Even so, in the late seventies the city was busy condemning them and moving the mostly elderly, predominately female, and all black residents into the projects' towers. The officials used words like "modern" and "renewal," "safety" and "the New South," but what they were really thinking about was a massive parking lot for the stadium.

Our project was to bring the houses up to city code before the inspectors could come and condemn them. My job was to convince the home owners that we weren't going to rob them, that we were, despite our race and youth, on their side. It was not an easy job, and I spent the first few weeks crying, unable to face the enormity of my inexperience and ignorance. I didn't want to quit, but I also didn't think I had it in me to persuade these people. I remained convinced of my inadequacy until I was taken in hand by an old woman named Miss Glover.

I never knew her first name, and like most everyone else who met her, I didn't have the nerve to ask her what it was. Weathered to a small thin reed, she was always dressed in muted shades of gray or all in black, with a porkpie hat perched at a jaunty angle on the back of her head. She was eighty years old when I first met her and she had just retired from her job as a maid for a family she said lived out in the country, about two miles outside the city limits. She latched onto the project as something to do with her considerable energy and because her neighbor's house had been bulldozed the year before and she didn't much appreciate the view from her dining room windows. The first day I met her she squeezed my upper arm and said, "Child, don't you have a mother?"

I said I had a pretty good one and she just shook her head. "Then I hope she don't see you till I get through with you."

The next day when I came to work I found a small, exquisitely made coconut custard pie on my desk. My boss, a Methodist minister by the name of Houston Wheeler, told me it was from Miss Glover and that she had left instructions with the three men I worked with that it was specifically for me. They all knew Miss Glover well and were waiting for me to take the first piece, but after that they wanted their fair share. I portioned it out and as I bit into the sweet filling and cookie crust, I tried to figure out why she had made it for me. It wasn't my birthday and I hadn't done anything for her. There was just no reason other than she guessed I needed something to get me through the day and, on that score, the pie was just the thing. All through the morning, as I made my rounds of the neighborhood, I carried the proud feeling that some-one had done something special for me. That was the first day I didn't spend time in the bathroom crying, and the memory of it lasted into the following day as well.

As things shaped up and the people in the neighborhood grew accus-tomed to seeing a white Yankee girl ringing doorbells, I relaxed a bit. Over cups of coffee or iced tea, I'd tell people about the project and outline the repairs we could make. Over time I learned to sit back and listen to *them*. Partly it was the good teaching I received from Houston, but some of it, too, was due to Miss Glover and her two friends, Miss Annie Mae Baldwin and Miss Rose. Miss Rose was much younger than Miss Glover and much sprier than Miss Baldwin, who had horrible arthritis (though she still managed to clean houses three days a week), so sometimes Miss Rose came with me on my rounds. She'd introduce me around and tell me about the people I was meeting. Miss Baldwin did her share while sitting on her porch, stopping whoever passed by to point out the fine roof she got from us or to describe the plastering we had done in the parlor.

After the community began to accept our help more readily, my job included driving Miss Glover, Miss Baldwin, and Miss Rose to the city planning meetings and court hearings. The three of them knew most of the powerful white families in town, or knew of someone who had worked for them, and on the way back home, they would start planning how they'd use their contacts. If it was late, we would stop at a little home-cooking restaurant on the edge of the neighborhood, called Miss Julie's Kitchen, for coffee and something sweet ("Nothing like a bit of sweetness to send you off to sleep," Miss Baldwin would say). There the women would plan which of their former employers to call up and complain to about what the city was planning to do with the one thing they'd owned all their lives. Southerners, unlike people in the North, have a habit of staying rooted to where they were born. They also have long memories, and at one especially difficult juncture the women dredged up the ghost of one city official's relative, a person who had done something unspeakable during Reconstruction. They let the information slip into the ear of a sympathetic columnist at the *Atlanta Constitution* and he made good use of it. These methods—more than our project's intervention or the repairs we made—proved highly successful. One night, as I saw Miss Glover to her front door, I asked her if she felt bad about having to fight in such a sneaky way. She shook her head as if it were a foolish question and said, "This how it's been my whole life. They start out thinking you're nothing but a little cold tickling at their throats, so they don't pay you any attention until you bring them down so low they can't do nothing about it. But by then . . . well, I got what I want by then and I don't care what they think of me."

By the middle of the summer, the project had successfully blocked the city's plans for the neighborhood, and I realized that, as much as I cared about the people I worked for, I was never going to have the singular dedication of a good organizer. I was starting to understand that I needed to find a way to live that would allow me the time to put down on paper the stories I was slowly absorbing. I also wanted to be with Chris. Every month since Christmas, one of us had visited the other for a long weekend together. We have a series of photographs from one of those visits, taken in the kitchen of the house he shared with his newspaper's photographer. We are in the midst of making dinner and on the counter beside the open edition of *Joy of Cooking* are the fixings for breaded pork chops and a large glass bowl of cut peaches. Each shot advances the meal's preparation. In the last photo, Chris has fitted himself against my back and his arms follow mine down to the rolling pin where I am attempting to roll out the crust for a peach pie.

I had taken a bagful of peaches up to Ohio that I'd gathered from the trees on the lot beside Miss Glover's house where her neighbor's house once stood. The garden had somehow survived the bulldozer, and the two remaining peach trees blossomed that spring in a glorious frilly mass of pink flowers. We had turned the lot into a community garden and, around the end of July, the neighborhood ladies were feeding me all kinds of peach creations—cobblers, turnovers, jams, ham glazes, barbecue sauces. Miss Rose even made a facial mask from pulp and ground pits. ("That's a southern lady's secret," Miss Rose whispered to me. Then she added with a laugh, "Course, us that have beauty don't need that kind of stuff.") I don't really remember how well the peach pie I made for Chris turned out, but I do know from the date on the back of the photo that, when I got home that Sunday, Chris called me up and said it was time we got settled down.

I worked another month, then began to pack my bags. When I told Miss Glover my plans, she clasped my hands and asked me if I was sure I knew what I was doing.

"You don't have to marry a man to keep him around," she told me. It was no secret that she'd kept a few men busy in her time, and she was also up front with her opinion that, in general, she didn't have much use for men. I tried to assure her that I was doing the right thing, but she didn't believe me

Men and Pies

Most men have an intense relationship with pies. It's almost primal. Their face softens and their demeanor mellows at the mere mention of their favorite pie. In fact, it doesn't even have to be their favorite—they're happy with anything on a crust. It's all somehow tied up with their mother (even if their mother never touched a rolling pin in her life) and the association of pie with a warm, nurturing, safe environment. So formidable is the pie's power over the poor souls that I've come to think of pie—in all its varieties but particularly fruit and cream—as a potent aphrodisiac.

Try it. Lean close to someone whose attention you've been trying to grab and whisper, "Honey, I'm gonna make you a pie."

"Really?" he'll ask, maybe a little suspicious, yet intrigued. Then all you have to do is coo, "Just tell me what you like."

And you got him.

I once made the mistake at a party of stating my very strong conviction that pies are a perfect metaphor for the relationship between the sexes, wherefore women make them and men eat them, leaving little behind but crumbs and a messy plate.

I now admit I was wrong. Or at least that things are changing. Ever since that party men have gone out of their way to introduce themselves to me just to let me know that *they* make pies— not just occasionally but in large quantities and all the time.

I've also met the Pie Man, who stations himself in the Wall Street area of lower Manhattan to sell his assortment of fruit and custard pies. He is a youngish man who told me quite frankly that he thinks he's doing better work with a rolling pin than he ever did at a desk. From the look on the faces of the people who buy his pies and the way they lean against a nearby skyscraper to eat them, I believe he may be right.

There's also my neighbor Andy. My husband refers to Andy as the Lord High Mayor, not because he owns several houses on the block but because of his proud and handsome countenance. Andy is married to a woman who will tell you quite frankly that he's a trial to live with; he's a firm believer in the inalienable right of a man to be king in his own home. In no danger of ever having to live with him, I happen to be thoroughly in love with Andy. I look forward to seeing him each morning as we send our kids off to school before going to work. On summer nights, I sometimes sit with him on his stoop and listen to his stories. Usually we end up talking about cooking. He makes a magnificent paella, and nearly every Sunday, after working six and a half days at his shoe business, he bakes pies. Not just bakes pies, but invents pies with all kinds of crusts—he adds nuts, zest, different types of flour—and fillings. "You must come and have a taste of my apple-walnut" he calls to me from his yard, and I'm at his door in no time.

What I like most about men who bake their own pies is their passion about doing it. This is, I realize, a quality I want my own sons to have—not necessarily about baking pies but about something in life that is outside the traditional male sphere. Pies are a pretty good place to start. So the last time Sam asked me to make him one, I pulled out my rolling pin.

"Here," I said.

"What?" he asked, his fourteen-year-old voice cracking with slacker amazement.

"You can make one yourself."

"A pie?"

"Yeah, a pie."

"I don't know how to make a pie."

"I'll teach you."

"Can't you do it for me?"

I have trouble saying no to Sam. I look up into his beautiful, childlike face perched atop his already six-foot frame and see him as my firstborn, cradled in my arms. But this time I shook my head as I opened up a cookbook.

"You're almost a man. It's time you learned," I replied and walked away as, first with a stumble and moan but then with concentration and real enjoyment, he began to make his first pie.

and through the last week or two she quietly voiced her doubts. I had some doubts myself, but one thing I was certain about was that by marrying Chris I was going a long way toward understanding something that Miss Glover had made me aware of. Secure in a rich community of voices, regally embroidered in their history, Miss Glover and her friends had a connection to one another and the world around them that I could only long for. All the days and nights I'd spent with these women gave me a window to look through, the strength to push it open and lean upon the sill. Now I knew I had to go through it.

On my last full day in Atlanta, Miss Glover came to the office with another coconut custard pie. I was cleaning out the beat-up desk I used. There was no one else in the office. We sat down at the long table in the center of the room and, together, we ate every last crumb of the pie straight from the pan. When we were through and I had hugged her one last time, I watched her move slowly down the street toward her home, waving to just about everyone she saw. I thought it was hardly possible that I had ever been so warmly loved before; I still think that and am enriched each time I think of her.

A PIE YOU make to give to someone doesn't have to be terribly difficult, though some of the following recipes are a little involved. For that reason, when you tackle them, try to limit the distractions around you. That said, I'll confess that I've never quite managed to do this myself, and after many attempts at creating a cream filling while talking on the phone or answering my kids' questions, I've come to realize it can't be done. Usually the worst disasters happen when one of my sons decides he wants to talk to me about an Important Matter just as I'm measuring something. I am referring to the issues that are supposed to come up during our so-called quality time (not that I can identify which part of the day I spend with my children is the quality part) but more often than not come up when I'm holding a measuring cup. It's hard to remember how many teaspoons of cornstarch you've put into the sugar for a custard pie when you're being asked how to use a condom. (This discussion occurred after my sister—who works with women and children with AIDS—sent my oldest son a packet of teaching condoms and a couple of pamphlets on sexually transmitted diseases for the birthday that turned him into a teenager.)

My solution is to wait to start these kinds of pies until everyone's asleep. As a rule, I don't cook well with other people around—my kitchen is too small and I'm too scatterbrained. I find late night is the best time for making these more complicated pies. And since most of them require a setting period before either a topping is added or they are ready for eating, an overnight rest in the refrigerator is perfect. I put on some music, kick my shoes off, maybe even pour a glass of wine, then fall into the soothing rhythm of mixing and rolling. By the time the pie comes out of the oven, I'm exhausted and ready for bed. But I find I am also blessed with a strong sense of contentment, fed by my anticipation of the moment when I will present my gift.

Miss Glover's Coconut Custard Pie

*C*ustard pies are a trick you have to master. The main problem is that the crust, in order to be flaky, should be cooked at a high setting for a short period of time, while the custard demands a low, slow cooking. Miss Glover told me a trick about custard pies that I have seen mentioned elsewhere. You bake the crust and custard separately—the custard in a pie tin that's the exact same size and depth as the one for the crust. Then, while the custard is still warm (very important), you loosen it from the tin by running a butter knife around the edges, then tilt the tin over the crust and let the custard slip into the baked pie crust. This way you have a perfect crust *and* a perfect custard. It's easier than it seems, though I have sometimes ended up with a mess of custard instead of a perfect, unbroken surface. Try this method a couple of times and if the filling breaks, don't despair; you can cover up the broken custard with extra coconut shreds. If you're not up to this trick, use the following directions.

Single 9-inch Butter and Lard Crust (page 25), unbaked

Filling:
4 large eggs
^{2}/$_3$ cup sugar
^{1}/$_2$ teaspoon salt
2^2/$_3$ cups milk
1^1/$_2$ teaspoons vanilla extract
1 cup shredded coconut, preferably fresh
^{1}/$_4$ teaspoon ground nutmeg

1. Preheat the oven to 425°F.

2. Prepare the crust and set aside in the refrigerator while you make the filling.

3. In a large bowl, using an electric mixer, beat together the eggs, sugar, salt, milk, and vanilla until smooth. Stir in the coconut, then pour into the pie shell. Sprinkle the nutmeg on top.

4. Place the pie pan on top of a baking sheet or pizza pan and bake in the center of the oven for 15 minutes. Lower the heat to 350°F and bake for 25 to 30 minutes more or until a knife inserted into the edge of the custard comes out clean. The center may still be a little wobbly. Let the pie cool for at least 30 minutes before cutting.

S E R V E S   6.

Sweet Potato Pie

*T*his version is from a cookbook by Sheila Ferguson called *Soul Food*. What she says in her introduction is true: nearly everybody does have their own version of this great American pie. I do believe that, as great as a perfect apple pie can be, sweet potato pie is more satisfying—and more American. I started an argument about this when I once again stupidly opened my mouth at a party. The room quickly divided into those who favored apple pie and those who could not do without sweet potato pie. The people who came down on the side of sweet potato seemed to have the qualities I look for in friends—they were the warm ones with a good sense of humor—while the apple bunch were all straight-laced sourpusses. To be sure, there were quite a few at the gathering who thought we were all out of our minds. It was late and too many bottles of wine had already been drunk, but I, at least, remained serious. Sweet potato pie, and this version in particular, should be voted our national pie. This is the one pie I make for friends who, for one reason or another, need a hug.

Single 9-inch Butter and Lard Crust (page 25), unbaked

Filling:
3 cups warm mashed sweet potatoes
3 large eggs
1 cup sugar
¾ teaspoon salt
1½ teaspoons ground cinnamon
¾ teaspoon ground nutmeg
½ teaspoon ground allspice
1 cup heavy cream
Whipped cream, for serving (see Note)

1. Place a baking sheet on the middle rack of the oven and preheat the oven to 350°F.

2. Prepare the crust and set aside in the refrigerator while you make the filling.

3. In a large bowl, using an electric mixer, beat together the mashed sweet potatoes, eggs, sugar, salt, and spices. Pour in the cream and stir the mixture until it is very well blended.

4. Pour the mixture into the pie shell. Carefully transfer the pie pan to the baking sheet and bake for 1 hour or until a knife inserted in the middle of the pie comes out clean. Let the pie cool a little bit before topping with whipped cream and serving.

SERVES 6.

Note: Some recipes for sweet potato pie call for brandy or bourbon. They're nice touches but, given a choice, I'd add the liquor to the whipped cream any day. It is, of course, your duty to serve whipped cream with this pie.

Nancy's Lethal Pecan Pie Hangover Cure

I'm not making any claims for this pie. I was twenty when I last used it for medicinal purposes. Now when I make this pie, it's not as a cure but because it's so good.

Single 9-inch Butter and Lard Crust (page 25), unbaked

Filling:
1¼ cups dark corn syrup
1 cup firmly packed dark brown sugar
4 tablespoons (½ stick) unsalted butter
4 large eggs
1½ cups pecans, coarsely chopped
1 teaspoon vanilla extract

1. Preheat the oven to 350°F.

2. Prepare the crust and set aside in the refrigerator while you make the filling.

3. Put the corn syrup and sugar in a medium saucepan set over medium heat and stir until the sugar dissolves. Let the mixture boil softly for 2 minutes, then remove from the heat and stir in the butter.

4. In a large bowl, using an electric mixer, beat the eggs until they're light lemon in color. Continue beating while adding the sugar syrup. Stir in the pecans and vanilla.

5. Place the pie shell on a baking sheet or pizza pan. Pour the filling mixture into the pie shell and place in the center of the oven. Bake about 50 minutes, just until the filling is set.

SERVES 6.

Chocolate Pecan Pie

*M*iss Baldwin's niece copied this recipe for me from an old magazine. I use bittersweet instead of semisweet chocolate and less sugar to make it less cloyingly sweet. People's eyes always grow big when they take their first bite.

Single 9-inch Butter and Lard Crust (page 25), unbaked

Filling:
5 ounces bittersweet chocolate
1 cup light corn syrup
¹/₂ cup sugar
3 large eggs, lightly beaten
3 tablespoons unsalted butter, melted
2 teaspoons vanilla extract
1¹/₂ cups pecans, coarsely chopped
Sweetened whipped cream, for serving

1. Preheat the oven to 350°F.

2. Prepare the crust and set aside in the refrigerator while you make the filling.

3. In the top of a double boiler over hot, barely simmering water, melt the chocolate. Set aside to cool.

4. In a large bowl, stir together the corn syrup, sugar, eggs, butter, vanilla, and the cooled chocolate until well mixed. Add the pecans and mix well.

5. Pour the filling into the pie shell and bake for 50 to 55 minutes or until a knife inserted in the middle comes out clean. Let cool for as long as you can wait. Serve with a lot of sweetened whipped cream.

SERVES 6.

Plum Tart with Lemon Curd

*T*his pie is very juicy and the lemon curd seems to slap awake the plums to produce a truly vibrant dessert. Somehow this has settled in my mind as a holiday pie and I often make it at Christmas. Maybe it's because by then the plum season has ended and I have to go to a fancy market to get them. Or maybe it's the beautiful colors that merge on the crust. Whatever it is, this pie brings smiles to people's faces, especially in winter. It looks—and tastes—as though it is difficult to make, but it really isn't at all. This is a fairly large pie. It can be made in either a ten-inch shallow pie pan or an eleven-inch tart pan.

Single 11-inch Dessert Tart Crust (page 40), unbaked

Filling:
2 strips lemon zest
½ cup plus 2 tablespoons sugar
2 large eggs
1 large egg yolk
¼ cup fresh lemon juice
12 tablespoons (1½ sticks) unsalted butter
7 medium plums, pitted and quartered
½ cup plum jam

1. Preheat the oven to 350°F.

2. Prepare the crust and set aside in the refrigerator while you make the filling.

3. In a food processor fitted with the metal blade, process the lemon zest with ½ cup of the sugar until the zest is as fine as the sugar. Add the eggs, egg yolk, and lemon juice and process to combine.

4. Place the lemon mixture and the butter in the top of a double boiler set over simmering water and cook, stirring, until thick, about 6 minutes. Cover with plastic wrap and set aside to cool.

5. When cool, spread the lemon mixture over the bottom of the tart shell and top with the quartered plums, arranged in concentric circles, cut side down. Sprinkle with the remaining 2 tablespoons sugar and bake in the center of the oven for 35 to 40 minutes, until the rim is lightly golden and the plums are tender. Cool on a wire rack.

6. Melt the jam in a saucepan over low heat and brush over the cooled plums.

S E R V E S   8   T O   10.

Frozen Lemon Soufflé Pie

*H*ot August days scream for this pie. I place my slab of marble in the freezer the night before, then make the crust dough and go to bed. Early the next morning, I get up, roll the crust out on the ice-cold marble, and make the pie. By the time the day blazes out, the pie is ready to eat.

Depending on how sophisticated you want to this pie to be (and how much time you have), you can prebake either the All-Butter Crust or the Basic Cookie Crust. The butter crust is richer and more elegant. The cookie crust is less trouble and almost as good.

***Single 9-inch All-Butter Crust (page 26) or Basic Cookie Crust made
with vanilla wafers (page 36), baked***

Filling:
2 large eggs, separated
7 tablespoons sugar
Juice and finely grated zest of 2 large, dense lemons
1 cup heavy cream
Twists of lemon rind, for garnish

1. Prepare the crust of your choice.

2. In a large bowl, using an electric mixer, beat the egg yolks with 3 tablespoons of the sugar until the mixture is thick and lemony in color. Add the lemon juice and grated zest and continue beating until the mixture is smooth.

3. In another bowl, whip the cream with 2 tablespoons of the sugar until stiff. Fold in the yolk mixture.

4. In another bowl, beat the egg whites until soft peaks form. Continue to beat until very stiff and glossy, gradually adding the remaining 2 tablespoons sugar. Add to the whipped cream mixture and carefully fold until well mixed.

5. Gently pour the filling into the prepared pie shell. Cover the top with plastic wrap and freeze for at least 2 hours. When made with a cookie crust, this pie can last in the freezer for a month. (The short crust tends to wilt as it defrosts.) If you wish to freeze it, wrap the pie well in a double layer of plastic wrap.

6. Thirty minutes before serving, remove the pie from the freezer and place in the refrigerator. When ready to serve, garnish with thin twists of lemon rind.

S E R V E S 6.

Cappuccino Pie

Several years ago I found in a magazine a recipe for an enormous cappuccino chiffon dessert that was exceedingly delicious and equally arduous to make. I made it a couple of times, then lost the recipe. When my husband and the friends to whom I had served the dessert kept asking me to make it again, I figured out this pie version. It's infinitely less trouble to prepare but is still an impressive creation.

Single 9-inch Basic Cookie Crust made with chocolate wafers
(page 36), baked

Filling:
2 tablespoons instant espresso powder
1 envelope unflavored gelatin
½ cup milk
2 ounces unsweetened chocolate, chopped
½ cup sugar
3 large eggs, separated
¼ teaspoon salt
1 teaspoon vanilla extract
2 ounces bittersweet chocolate shavings
1 cup heavy cream
Ground cinnamon, for sprinkling

1. At least 4 hours before making the pie, place the instant espresso in a coffee filter and fit it over a measuring cup. Fill it with 1 cup boiling water, cover, and let sit for 4 hours or, even better, overnight.

2. Prepare the crust.

3. When ready to make the pie, gently pick up the coffee filter and squeeze it like a tea bag to get all the coffee liquid into the measuring cup. Set aside.

4. Sprinkle the gelatin over the coffee and let stand a few minutes to allow the gelatin to soften.

5. In a medium saucepan, combine the milk and unsweetened chocolate. Place over low heat and cook, stirring constantly, until the chocolate melts. Remove from the heat and add ¼ cup of the sugar, the egg yolks, and salt. Whisk until blended.

6. Return the saucepan to the heat and cook, stirring constantly, until the mixture thickens slightly and just reaches a simmer. Do not boil.

7. Add the gelatin-coffee mixture to the chocolate mixture and stir over the heat about a minute longer. Pour the mixture into a bowl and refrigerate until it mounds when dropped from a spoon, about 1 hour. (You can speed up this step by placing the bowl in a large bowl of ice, then placing them both in the freezer. However, you have to be careful that the mixture doesn't freeze. Check after 15 minutes.)

8. Remove the chocolate mixture from the refrigerator and stir in the vanilla.

9. In a medium bowl, using an electric mixer, beat the egg whites until soft peaks form. Slowly add the remaining ¼ cup sugar and continue beating until stiff peaks form. Gently fold into the chocolate mixture. Pour into the cool baked pie shell and chill overnight until set.

10. Sprinkle the filling with the chocolate shavings.

11. Whip the cream with an electric mixer until stiff peaks form. Mound gently on top of the chocolate mixture, spreading carefully to the edges of the crust. Sprinkle cinnamon over the whipped cream. Serve at once.

S E R V E S 6.

Tiramisù Pie

The original tiramisù recipe on which this pie is based belongs to the mother of my niece's boyfriend. Carla and her son, Alessio, live in Florence, where Meghan met him when she was studying politics for her undergraduate degree. She returned home to graduate and a few months later went back, this time, she said, to study French. She's still over there, studying French in Florence. As a good mother, my sister, Sue, recently went over to see what was happening with her daughter. She spent a very nice week visiting with Alessio's family and touring Florence. More importantly, she spent time with her daughter, who, she found out, *is* actually studying French and has a general plan for her life that is separate from being in Florence with Alessio. When Sue was about to leave, Alessio's mother gave her the family recipe for tiramisù, which, she was told by Meghan, is a family secret.

Sue brought a big dish of it to Easter dinner at my house. After dinner, we were sitting around the table scraping the bowl when it came to us that it might make a pretty good pie. I think it does.

The recipe makes two nine-inch pies or one eleven-inch pie with a little filling left over to eat all by itself.

Crust:
1 (16-ounce) package Savoiardi biscuits (see Note)
8 tablespoons (1 stick) unsalted butter, melted

Filling:
5 large eggs, separated
3 tablespoons sugar
5 tablespoons cognac
16 ounces mascarpone cheese

³/₄ cup strong espresso
¹/₄ cup almond-flavored liqueur
Dutch cocoa, for dusting

1. Preheat the oven to 350°F.

2. In the bowl of a food processor fitted with the metal blade, process 24 of the biscuits until they are fine crumbs. Pour the melted butter through the feed tube and pulse 2 or 3 times until the crumbs are moist.

3. Press the crumbs into 2 deep 9-inch pie pans or a single 11-inch pie pan and bake in the center of the oven for 8 to 10 minutes, until the crust is set. Set aside to cool while you make the filling.

4. In a large bowl, using an electric mixer, beat the egg yolks with the sugar until the eggs are a light lemon color. Add the cognac and beat to mix. Add the mascarpone and beat until well mixed.

5. In a separate bowl, using an electric mixer, beat the egg whites until stiff peaks form. Fold into the mascarpone mixture.

6. Combine the espresso and liqueur in a soup bowl. Pour a thin layer of the mascarpone mixture into the prepared pie crust(s). One at a time, dip the remaining biscuits into the espresso and arrange in a pinwheel pattern on the surface of the mascarpone. Cover the biscuits with another layer of mascarpone and dust the top with cocoa.

7. Refrigerate until set, at least 4 hours but preferably overnight.

A   S I N G L E   9 - I N C H   P I E   S E R V E S   6 .

Note: Savoiardi biscuits are just fancy ladyfingers, though they come from Italy, which adds some authenticity to the recipe. Don't get hung up, though: if you can't get this particular brand, use whatever kind of ladyfingers you can find.

Flaming Peach Pie

*T*his pie makes a most impressive entrance. I have served it for birthdays and the Fourth of July.

Single 9-inch All-Butter Crust (page 26), unbaked

Filling:
¹/₂ cup plus 1 tablespoon all-purpose flour
7 to 10 ripe peaches, peeled, pitted, and cut in half
¹/₄ cup firmly packed light brown sugar
4 tablespoons (¹/₂ stick) unsalted butter, at room temperature
¹/₂ teaspoon ground nutmeg
2 tablespoons light rum

1. Preheat the oven to 400°F.

2. Prepare the crust and rub 1 tablespoon of the flour over the bottom of the shell.

3. Arrange the peach halves over the bottom of the pastry, building them up slightly toward the center.

4. In a small bowl, blend together the brown sugar, the remaining ¹/₂ cup flour, the butter, and nutmeg until crumbly. Sprinkle the mixture over the peaches.

5. Bake in the center of the oven for 30 to 35 minutes or until the pastry is golden brown and the topping is crisp. Remove from the oven and carry to the table to serve.

6. Warm the rum in a small saucepan and sprinkle over the top of the pie. Ignite immediately and serve as soon as the flames go out.

SERVES 6.

Peach Melba Ice Cream Pie

*T*his is a very beautiful pie that my sister and I make for one another at the drop of a hat, and often when one of us feels the other needs a little extra attention.

The crust for this pie is a little unusual. It's a nut crust that is made very moist and chewy with coconut. It's very important to use the freshest coconut you can find.

Crust:
1 (3½-ounce) can sweetened flaked coconut
¼ cup finely chopped walnuts
2 tablespoons unsalted butter, melted

Filling:
1 quart good peach ice cream, slightly softened
1 pint good vanilla ice cream, slightly softened

Sauce:
2 cups skinned, sliced fresh peaches, soaked for at least 1 hour in
orange-flavored liqueur (quantity depends on both your
taste and mood, but at least ¼ cup)
½ cup sugar
1 tablespoon cornstarch
2 pints fresh raspberries

1. Preheat the oven to 325°F.

2. To make the crust, in a small bowl toss together the coconut, walnuts, and butter. Press the mixture firmly and evenly against the bottom and sides of a 9-inch pie pan.

3. Bake for 10 to 15 minutes or until the crust is golden brown. Remove from the oven and cool completely.

4. To make the filling, spoon the peach ice cream into the cooled crust, pressing down on the ice cream and spreading it to the edges of the crust. Then spoon the vanilla ice cream over the peach ice cream. Wrap in plastic and freeze.

5. To make the sauce, drain the liquid from the peaches into a medium saucepan and reserve the slices. Add the sugar and cornstarch to the peach liquid and cook over medium heat until the sauce thickens slightly. Boil 2 minutes more. Gently stir in the raspberries, remove from the heat, and set aside to cool. Taste to see if you need to add more liqueur.

6. Just before serving, arrange the peach slices over the top of the pie in a pretty circle. Cut a wedge and pour the raspberry sauce over it.

S E R V E S   4   T O   6.

The Best Lemon Meringue Pie

*A*ll meringue-topped pies should be eaten in one sitting. That's what makes them such perfect treats. Within twenty-four hours after they're cut, the meringue begins to separate from the edges of the crust and turns dewy. The filling, too, begins to shift, and though it may still be delicious it's not nearly the lovely confection it was the day before.

Of all meringue-topped pies, lemon seems to be the favorite. You need a fairly strong crust to hold up to the moist filling, so I use Betty's Pie Crust.

Single 9-inch Betty's Pie Crust (page 24), baked

Filling:
1¼ cups sugar
6 tablespoons cornstarch
2 cups water
3 large egg yolks
⅓ cup fresh lemon juice
3 tablespoons unsalted butter

Meringue:
3 large egg whites
Good pinch cream of tartar
4 to 6 tablespoons sugar

1. Prepare the crust.

2. To make the filling, combine the sugar and cornstarch in the top of a double boiler. Stir in the water.

3. In a medium bowl, using an electric mixer, beat together the yolks and lemon juice until the mixture is light yellow in color. Add to the sugar mixture. Cook over gently boiling water, stirring occasionally, until thick, a good 25 minutes. Stir in the butter. Pour into the pie shell and cover the top of the filling with plastic wrap. Cool in the refrigerator for at least an hour.

4. Preheat the oven to 350°F.

5. To make the meringue, in a large bowl, using an electric mixer, beat the egg whites until medium peaks form. Add the cream of tartar and continue to beat. As the peaks get stiffer, begin to add the sugar, 1 tablespoon at a time, until the meringue is as sweet as you want it to be. Beat until the meringue is very stiff and glossy but does not look dry.

6. Peel the plastic wrap off the lemon filling. Spoon the meringue over the lemon surface, mounding toward the center and coming all the way to the edges of the crust. Form peaks and curls by flipping the back of the spoon over the surface of the meringue. For added beauty, sprinkle the surface lightly with sugar.

7. Bake in the center of the oven for 10 minutes or until the top is lightly browned.

SERVES 6.

Individual Berry Shortcake Pies

*A*n old southern version of New England shortcake. I sometimes make a stack of Short Crust Pastry circles and freeze them. Wrapped tightly, they'll keep for a month or two. When ready to serve, defrost them slowly. Any fruit you have on hand will do nicely for the filling. An interesting idea, especially in winter, is to mix a couple of lightly poached fruits together, such as apples and pears.

4 individual Short Crust Pastry circles (page 34), baked

Filling:
1 pint fresh berries
1½ cups heavy cream, whipped and sweetened to taste

1. Prepare the pastry.

2. Cut any large berries, such as strawberries, into smaller chunks, reserving a few whole ones to use as garnishes. Fold the fruit into the whipped cream.

3. To serve, mound the filling on top of the shortcake circles. Garnish with whole berries.

MAKES 4 INDIVIDUAL PIES.

Two-Cheese Cheesecake Pie

*I*f you double this recipe and use a springform pan, you have one of the best cheesecakes around. And it serves sixteen people! My older son, Sam, kept after me to make a cheesecake when I wasn't having a house full of company and so I figured out how to make this pie.

Single 9-inch Basic Graham Cracker Crust
(page 36), unbaked

Filling:
18 ounces cream cheese, at room temperature
and cut into cubes
½ cup small-curd cottage cheese
2 large eggs
½ cup sugar
1 teaspoon vanilla extract
¼ cup sour cream

1. Preheat the oven to 350°F and place a baking sheet on the center rack of the oven.

2. Press the crust onto the bottom and up the sides of a 9-inch, lightly oiled, deep-dish pie pan. The bottom should be a good thickness, the sides thinner. Set aside.

3. In the bowl of a food processor fitted with the metal blade, process the cream cheese until smooth, about 40 seconds, scraping down the sides of the work bowl as needed.

4. Add the cottage cheese and process until smooth, about 30 seconds. Add the eggs and sugar and pulse to blend. Add the vanilla and sour cream and pulse to blend, scraping down the bowl as needed.

5. Slowly pour the filling into the prepared pie pan. Place the pan on the baking sheet in the preheated oven and bake until the edges of the filling have risen slightly and are firm to the touch, about 40 minutes.

6. Cool completely. Cover and refrigerate for at least 3 hours before serving.

SERVES 6 TO 8.

Black Forest Cherry Cheesecake Pie

*A*n elegant variation on Two-Cheese Cheesecake Pie (page 231).

Single 9-inch Basic Graham Cracker Crust
(page 36), unbaked

Filling:
1¼ pounds cream cheese, at room temperature
and cut into cubes
2 large eggs
1 cup sugar
2 teaspoons vanilla extract
½ cup canned sour cherries, drained and patted dry
4½ ounces bittersweet chocolate, melted
Chocolate shavings, for garnish

1. Preheat the oven to 350°F and place a baking sheet on the center rack of the oven.

2. Press the crust onto the bottom and up the sides of a 9-inch, lightly oiled, deep-dish pie pan. The bottom should be a good thickness, the sides thinner. Set aside.

3. In a food processor fitted with the metal blade, process the cream cheese until smooth, about 40 seconds, scraping down the bowl as needed.

4. Add the eggs, sugar, and vanilla to the cream cheese and process for 20 seconds.

5. Place about ⅔ cup of the cream cheese mixture in a small bowl and stir in the cherries.

6. Whisk the melted chocolate into the remaining cream cheese mixture and pour about three-quarters of it into the prepared pie pan, smoothing the top. Carefully spoon the cherry mixture over it and cover with the remaining cream cheese—chocolate mixture. Smooth the top.

7. Place the pan on the baking sheet in the preheated oven and bake until the edges of the filling have risen slightly and are firm to the touch but the center is still soft, about 35 minutes.

8. Cool completely. Cover and refrigerate for at least 4 hours before serving. Garnish with chocolate shavings.

SERVES 6 TO 8.

Angel Pie

I've seen versions of this recipe in dog-eared church pamphlets and crumbling ladies' magazines. I even found a copy in a dusty index box of recipes that my mother-in-law kept in her cupboard. She claimed she made it once and then, like a lot of things having to do with cooking, she never touched it again.

I incorporate finely chopped nuts—usually almonds or pistachios—into the meringue crust for added interest. I also add lime juice to the whipped cream. It undercuts the sweetness of the meringue and the filling and gives the pie a much-needed tartness.

Crust:
4 large egg whites
¼ teaspoon cream of tartar
1 cup sugar
½ cup finely chopped nuts, such as almonds, pistachios, or hazelnuts

Filling:
4 large egg yolks
½ cup sugar
¼ cup fresh lime juice
1 tablespoon freshly grated lime zest
¼ teaspoon salt
1 cup heavy cream, whipped

1. Preheat the oven to 300°F.

2. Slightly heat a 9-inch glass pie pan in the oven (about 5 minutes), then remove and spray with nonstick cooking spray and wipe with a paper towel. Set aside.

3. In a large bowl, using an electric mixer, beat the egg whites until they form soft peaks. Sprinkle the cream of tartar over the peaks and beat some more, gradually adding the sugar. Continue beating until the egg whites form stiff peaks. Carefully fold in the nuts. Spread the meringue evenly in the prepared pan.

4. Bake for 1 hour without opening the oven door. After the hour, take a peek and if the crust is a pale yellow, turn off the oven and leave the door slightly open. Leave the pie in the oven to cool for at least an hour. Transfer to the refrigerator and chill thoroughly.

5. Beat the yolks in the top of a double boiler. Add the sugar, lime juice and zest, and salt. Place over slowly boiling water and cook, stirring constantly, until thick enough to coat the back of a wooden spoon. Remove from the heat, cover the surface with plastic wrap, and chill.

6. Spread half of the whipped cream into the meringue shell, leaving about an inch around the perimeter creamless. Spread the filling over the cream, then top with the remaining whipped cream, mounding in the center and spreading with the back of a spoon to the edges.

7. Chill for at least 4 hours before serving.

SERVES AT LEAST 6.

Chocolate Chiffon Pie

*T*his recipe comes from my sister's friend John, who works with her at an AIDS clinic for women and children. He confessed to me that some days he drives to the supermarket straight from work, picks up enough ingredients for a couple of these pies, and goes directly home to make them. His wife finds him later with at least half of one already gone, and though the kitchen is a mess and he complains of a slightly sticky feeling in his bones, he still claims this pie is like a down comforter: he falls into it, he says, and wraps himself in its richness.

Single 9-inch Basic Cookie Crust made with vanilla or chocolate wafers (page 36), baked

Filling:
1 envelope unflavored gelatin
1 cup brewed coffee
½ cup milk
2 ounces unsweetened chocolate, chopped
½ cup sugar
3 large eggs, separated
¼ teaspoon salt
1 teaspoon vanilla extract
1 cup heavy cream

1. Prepare the crust.

2. Sprinkle the gelatin over the coffee in a small saucepan and let stand for a few minutes. In a medium saucepan over low heat, combine the milk and chocolate and cook, stirring constantly, until the chocolate melts. Remove from the heat and add ¼ cup of the sugar, the egg yolks, and salt and stir until mixed. Return to the heat and cook until the mixture thickens slightly, stirring constantly, about 5 minutes. Don't boil.

3. Place the gelatin-coffee mixture over low heat until the gelatin has melted. Pour into the chocolate mixture, stir, and refrigerate, stirring now and then, until it mounds softly, about 1 hour. Add the vanilla.

4. In a medium bowl, using an electric mixer, whip the cream until stiff. In another bowl, whip the egg whites until soft peaks form. Slowly add the remaining ¼ cup sugar to the egg whites and continue beating until stiff peaks form. Fold the cream into the egg whites, then gently but completely stir into the chocolate mixture. Pour into the prepared crust, mounding the filling toward the center. Chill for several hours if you possibly can.

SERVES 6.

Lena's Chocolate Pie with Nuts

I got this recipe from my brother, who was sent it by his brother-in-law's wife's mother, who is from Baton Rouge. She noted at the bottom of the recipe that Lena was her great-grandmother's housekeeper. Her grandmother raised two small granddaughters after her daughter died and also ran a busy family business, so Lena took over much of the cooking. Nearly a hundred years later, Lena's chocolate pie is still a nourishing and cherished family memory. See page 28 for instructions to partially bake crust.

Single 9-inch Butter and Lard Crust (page 25), partially baked

Filling:
3 large eggs, separated
4 tablespoons cornstarch
1½ cups milk
1 cup sugar
2 tablespoons Dutch cocoa
1 tablespoon unsalted butter, at room temperature
1 cup finely chopped pecans, plus extra for garnish

1. Prepare the crust.

2. In a medium saucepan, combine the egg yolks, cornstarch, milk, sugar, and cocoa and cook over medium heat, stirring constantly, until thickened—the mixture should coat the back of the spoon. Remove from the heat and add the butter. Stir until the butter is completely mixed in.

3. Add the pecans and pour into the pie shell. Cover the filling with a piece of plastic wrap and refrigerate until set, about 3 hours or overnight.

4. Preheat the oven to 350°F.

5. Beat the egg whites until very stiff and glossy. Take the plastic wrap off the pie filling and smooth the egg whites over the top, making peaks with the back of your spoon.

6. Bake in the center of the oven for 25 to 30 minutes or until the meringue is set and the peaks are nicely browned.

7. Sprinkle any extra pecans on top.

SERVES 6.

Blueberry–Whipped Cream Pie

*I*f I remember to, I freeze a couple pints of blueberries before they are gone from the market. Then, early on a hot summer morning, I make this pie and refrigerate it until very late at night. Then, around midnight, Chris and I sit on the cool iron steps that lead down into our garden with the pie plate between us and slowly work our way through the pie while our neighbors' air conditioners whirl and drip and the night melts about us.

Single 9-inch Butter and Lard Crust (page 25), baked

Filling:
1 pint fresh blueberries
²/₃ cup sugar (a little more if blueberries are very tart or
you have a sweet tooth)
2 tablespoons cornstarch
²/₃ cup boiling water
2 tablespoons unsalted butter
1¹/₂ tablespoons fresh lemon juice
1 cup heavy cream
2 tablespoons confectioners' sugar
Whipped cream or ice cream, for serving (optional)

1. Prepare the crust.

2. Pick over the berries and wash and drain well. Place in a large bowl.

3. In a medium saucepan, combine the sugar, cornstarch, and boiling water. Add 1 cup of the blueberries and stir gently over medium heat until the mixture comes to a boil and becomes thick, about 3 to 4 minutes.

4. Remove from the heat and stir in the butter and lemon juice. Cool slightly, then fold the mixture into the rest of the blueberries. Cover and refrigerate until cold but not set.

5. About an hour before serving, in a large bowl, using an electric mixer, whip the cream until thick. Add the confectioners' sugar and continue beating until stiff peaks form. Spread the cream over the bottom of the pie shell, spreading it up high on the sides. Pour the blueberry filling over the cream, spreading it gently into an even layer.

6. Refrigerate until ready to serve. Make more whipped cream or serve with slightly melted ice cream if you're not watching your weight.

S E R V E S 6.

Sweet Dreams

Health is the first muse, and sleep is the condition to produce it.

—RALPH WALDO EMERSON, *UNCOLLECTED LECTURES*

I am a firm believer that you must make a good lamb stew on the first cold night of October and that a small martini (made with Boodles gin, if possible) and a large bowl of saffron consommé brewed from a strong veal stock will go a long way toward curing the common cold. I also believe that a slice of leftover apple pie, heated through and surrounded by a puddle of warm heavy cream, is the best remedy for sleeplessness.

I believe this about apple pie because I am so often the beneficiary of its medicinal powers. I fool a lot of people—even those I live with—because most nights I'm in bed by ten, fast asleep by eleven. My husband and sons make fun of me when I start drooping soon after dinner—the one period in the day when it's hard for me to concentrate on much of anything. So I wave off their comments about the early hour and go on to bed, hearing their voices in the rooms below as I drift into sleep. Chris reports that when he finally slips in beside me, except for a few snorts, there is no sign of life in me. He pats my head, adjusts the covers around my shoulders, and, secure in the knowledge that the household is bedded down safely for the night, soon falls into his own deep and undisturbed rest.

At about two o'clock, my eyes open and my head starts filling with unwanted thoughts while my body thrums with lists of things I have to do. I attempt to empty my brain, to tell my body this is no time to be up. If it doesn't listen, I try to recall some of the things I was supposed to have learned in yoga—and further back, in Lamaze classes—about quiet breathing and relaxation techniques. When these don't work—and these days they often don't— I finally give up and go downstairs.

When I was younger I used to take my bike out and ride through the deserted streets around my parents' home in Philadelphia. I knew every corner of my neighborhood. It was intoxicating to tear through the dark stillness, trespassing across lawns and alleys, careening around the prim exteriors of slumbering houses. Even in Ravenna, I would slip away from Chris's arms to race my bike down country roads and pitch-black farm lanes. These moments of edgy nocturnal wakefulness were rare in those days and seemed more a gift than anything else. I rode for miles and when I came back, my body exhausted, I dove into a deep, rich sleep and was, the following day, infused with a powerful sense of contentment.

Things are different now. My wakeful nights have grown more frequent and I have become resentful of their intrusion. I know as I leave the warmth of my husband's side that I'm going to be tired during the day. It would help, I know, if I could do something as physically tiring as riding my bike again. It would quiet the jumble of noise in my brain and relieve the jitters along my spine, but Brooklyn can be inhospitable to late-night wanderings. So sometimes I try to work, often I read, but usually I end up just standing at the kitchen door, caught by the darkened shroud of the surrounding yards and the old whitewashed walls of our neighbors' houses. It's comforting to see a couple of lights on, and I have come to know a few of my neighbors by their silhouettes

in the blue haze of TV screens. The woman in the house catty-corner to my garden calls to her dogs to come in in a heavy brogue (I know their names—Lilly
and Bobo—but not hers) at about the same time that a young Asian man gets
dressed for work by the light of a single bare bulb in a narrow room fitted with
a loft bed and decorated with movie posters. A soft red glow from a shrine to
Krishna emanates from the sill of a house four doors up where once in the summer I watched an old woman wash her long gray hair under the garden hose in
the yard. Afterward, she wound herself into a yellow sari of such delicate mate-
rial it appeared to float around her body like a vaporous cloud. On even the
clearest of nights, the foghorn in the harbor will occasionally blare. When the
bells of the Basilica of Our Lady of Perpetual Help at the top of our street strike
the hour, the two sounds join together, vibrating out over the stillness that so
briefly falls across the city just as the morning light begins to drain the sky.

These days, when I make an apple pie, it is with this moment in mind.
What my family leaves after they've had their dessert I grab in the night and,
perched on a stool in the kitchen with my dog Brendan (who feels it's his duty
to be within a foot of me at all times) by my side, I eat a few forkfuls. If this is
just a blip of wakefulness, I will eat it right out of the pie tin, breaking off some
of the crust to give to Brendan in thanks for his company. But if I know this will
be a harder case, I'll cut out a good slice, put it on a plate, and heat it in the
oven. Some people might layer cheese on top to melt but, to me, that's an afternoon affectation. The dead of night calls for cream, perhaps fortified, as my
mother would have it, with a tablespoon or two of brandy.

Packed in the Pilgrims' baggage to remind them in Plymouth of their
homeland, apple spurs quickly bloomed into a symbol of our collective American soul. In 1848, Ralph Waldo Emerson wrote in his journal, "The apple is
our national fruit and I like to see that the soil yields it; I judge of the country
so. The American sun paints himself in these glowing balls amid the green
leaves." A few years later, as the Civil War boiled up, Henry Ward Beecher

preached that our country must, like the best apple pie, "become a glorious unity in which sugar gives up its nature as sugar and butter ceases to be butter and each flavoursome spice gladly vanishes from its own full nature, that all of them by a common death, may rise into the new life of an apple pie . . . transformed [into] the ideal, refined, purified and by fire fixed in blissful perfection."

If not always considered in such fancy terms as Beecher's, the apple tree continued to help transform the land. We Americans took the tree everywhere we went, its fruit dried and stored in barrels to sustain us across the Great Plains, its branches wrapped in burlap to plant on the far shores of the Pacific. Secured by legends and folklore, apple pie is fixed in our American hearts. A few years back, the nursery school that both Sam and Al attended was giving a benefit dinner to raise money for books and school supplies. Each family was to cook a turkey (chosen because the director got a good deal from a local butcher) and also something for dessert. The population of the school reflected the changes in the neighborhood; no longer predominately Hispanic with a smattering of white kids, there were now Asian, Indian, Mexican, Middle Eastern, and Eastern European children as well, all fairly new not just to the neighborhood but to the country. The turkeys were made into *moles*, smoked in tea leaves, minced into stews, slathered with curry spices, and wrapped in banana leaves, but what most parents chose for dessert were apple pies, some store-bought, others homemade.

One of the mothers, a woman who had come from Hong Kong two years earlier and had opened a restaurant on a block that was being transformed from a forlorn stretch of abandoned storefronts into a bustling market of fresh fruit and fish stands, told me she bought seven magazines before she found just the right recipe.

"I use my kind of apples," she said proudly as she held up one of the most beautiful pies I've ever seen.

"What kind is that?" I asked.

"I don't know what you call them. But you come and I'll show you."

I walked by her restaurant a few months later, and though it was snowing and miserable out, she pulled me to a nearby stall and pointed out a large tan fruit, speckled green—what we have named an Asian pear apple, a sharp, crisp fruit with a sweet bite to its juice. The next time I made an apple pie, I used it and found, as Beecher would have said, that it gave up its unique qualities to enrich in a subtly strong way the whole.

As I sit in my small chilly kitchen eating my piece of pie and hoping, soon, for sleep, I sometimes think about my Uncle Frank and something I heard him say once. What has rubbed me awake I think is what he used to refer to as "the itch." He was my father's oldest brother and though I can't recall ever exchanging more than a few words with him at a time, I maintain a warm place for him in my heart. A man of varied and strong talents, he was on his way to the major leagues from a starring position as a second baseman in the minors when the beer he drank with his teammates after the games caught up with him. When he drank, my dad said, Uncle Frank's shyness and awkwardness left him and he became what he was inside, a brilliant, funny, and emotionally generous man. His post-baseball years are not much mentioned in the family, partly because watching a beloved brother stumble out of their reach still haunts my father and aunts, but also because, as drinkers themselves, the riddle of why Uncle Frank fell from grace seems so mysterious. One of the reasons I didn't get to know Uncle Frank until I was older was that when he quit drinking and began to rebuild his life, he stopped coming to family parties, avoiding anything that might cause him to slip. He was not among the uncles who joked around the washing machine filled with beer and he did not add his voice to those who sat at the kitchen table telling stories about the war and growing up poor on the city's streets.

Instead he'd come to our house late at night. After he retired from his position as a chemist at a paint factory, he took a part-time job as a security guard on the graveyard shift to keep himself busy. Before work or on his days off he'd visit not only his sisters and my dad, but all the more far-flung relatives in New England and Maryland. When my mother saw his car pull up, she'd start a fresh pot of coffee and put out a plate of food. He walked into the house very fast, with the attending-to-business-needing-to-be-done air of a workman, and come to rest on the edge of a kitchen chair, jangling one of his long legs nervously before him. He had the same fine features and balding head as my dad. They sat across from one another like bookends and talked about things that sounded unimportant to me then but that I now see were the codes they used to let each other know how they were both doing—the emotional dialogue of two men deficient in the language of love. In what seemed like only a few minutes, Uncle Frank would drain the last of the coffee in the pot, then give in to my mom's plea to play something on our piano. If my sister and brother and I weren't hanging around, she'd call to us to come downstairs or, if it was really late, we would wake in our beds to the sounds of one of Beethoven's piano sonatas. Huddled on the steps with my brother and sister, I'd watch my uncle play, his thin back hunched low over the keys, his face set hard in concentration. A few notes more, then a sharp bang in midphrase and he was out the door while the last notes still vibrated through the piano's belly.

"Gotta go," he'd reply to my mother's begging that he stay and play some more. "Got the itch to go."

If I were to leave this house in the middle of the night, I don't know where I would go. Maybe, like Uncle Frank, I would tear down the turnpike to my parents, my sister or brother, or keep on going farther, down south to friends I haven't seen in years, to my aunt who is a nun and loves to cook in the huge kitchen of an old retreat house that hangs precariously over the ocean on the Jersey shore. I am the same age now as my uncle was when he regained his life. At times, especially late at night when memories flare up with all the beautiful mayhem of a brushfire seen across a flat plain, I feel the breath of early promises that were not fulfilled, the rub of mistakes, and the price of disappointments.

We are a nation of people fleeing from some kind of trouble or another, in search of fertile soil to plant another dream. It makes us different and is, perhaps, the source of whatever greatness we might possess, that something was given up, torn away, and from whatever remained, a new life was made. It is what my uncle did when his early were dreams destroyed. It was his itch, the need to continue on, making what he could with what he could salvage. In his travels at night, I believe my uncle struggled from a warring past to a vision of a peaceful future. This is not unlike what the Pilgrims must have felt when they unwrapped the branches they had uprooted from their homeland and planted the green shoots in unfamiliar soil in the hope of making for themselves a better life.

I finish my piece of pie, and Brendan and I make the rounds that Chris made earlier. We check the doors, stand beside Sam's bed first, then Al's, and tuck in whatever wayward limb juts from the covers. Then I soundlessly return to my own bed, slide under the covers, careful to keep my cold feet away from Chris even as I curl close to him and reach a hand under his pillow to touch his. I can still taste the sweetness of the apples in my mouth; the warm pastry and cream batten the thoughts in my head. Here, at last, is a measure of peace. There are roads to travel, troubles to overcome, but for now, there is only a sigh as I drift, deeply and at last, to sleep.

THERE ARE ABOUT as many ways to make an apple pie as there are cooks in our country. These eight are my favorite.

A Common Apple Pie

*T*his is my recipe for a straightforward apple pie. It reflects not only my preferences but also countless influences. It is intentionally imprecise because there are so many variables to consider. To get it right, you pretty much have to taste as you go along or trust your instincts.

Double 9-inch Butter and Lard Crust (page 25), unbaked

Filling:
8 or 9 large apples of several different cooking varieties (Delicious apples
will NOT do), peeled, cored, and thinly sliced
Juice of 1 large lemon
Sugar
Ground cinnamon
Pinch of both ground mace and ground nutmeg
Unsalted butter
1 large egg white beaten with a little water, for brushing

1. Preheat the oven to 450°F.

2. Prepare the pastry. Line a 9-inch pie pan with half of the pastry and set aside in the refrigerator, along with the unrolled half, while you make the filling.

3. Taste a few slices of the apples to gauge how much sugar you'll need to make them sweet. In a large bowl, mix the apple slices with the lemon juice. Sprinkle with sugar and cinnamon to taste, then add the mace and nutmeg.

4. Pour the apple mixture into the prepared pastry shell. Mound toward the center and dot with butter.

5. Roll out the remaining pastry and carefully lay it over the apples. Seal the edges, cut

vent holes, and decorate with extra pieces of dough cut into decorative shapes. Brush the egg wash over the surface of the pastry.

6. Place the pie pan on a baking sheet (to catch any spillover) and cook in the middle of the oven for 10 minutes. Turn the oven down to 350°F and continue to cook for about another hour, until the top crust is a beautiful golden brown. If the edges start to darken too much, cover with a ribbon of aluminum foil.

SERVES 6.

Variations

*E*veryone has their own way with apple pie, but here are a few of the traditional variations, plus a sauce to pour on top.

Dutch: Omit dotting the apples with butter. Five minutes before the pie is finished baking, pour about $\frac{1}{2}$ cup heavy cream through the vents in the top crust. Return to the oven and complete baking.

Crumb: Omit the top crust. Mix together $\frac{1}{2}$ cup firmly packed light brown sugar, 1 cup all-purpose flour, and $\frac{1}{2}$ cup sugar to form crumbs and sprinkle over the top of the unbaked pie. Bake the pie as instructed.

Apple-Cheese: Arrange slices of good sharp cheddar cheese over the apples before putting on the top crust. Another alternative is to sprinkle grated cheddar cheese in the bottom of the crust before you pour in the apples.

Apple-Raisin: Add about $\frac{1}{3}$ cup raisins (more or less to taste) to the apple filling.

Sundae Sauce for Apple Pie: In a medium saucepan, mix together $\frac{1}{2}$ cup light brown sugar, $\frac{1}{4}$ cup light corn syrup, $1\frac{1}{2}$ teaspoons ground cinnamon, and 1 tablespoon unsalted butter. Bring to a boil over low heat. Serve warm.

Apple Custard Pie

This is one of the few things I remember my grandmother making for us in the short time that she lived with us. She was tall and even though she was in her late seventies at the time, she held her back very erect. Her mind was nearly gone and often she confused me and my sister (I was six and Sue was almost ten) with girlfriends she had had in Ireland. For hours on end, she would sit in her bedroom, which was next to ours, and call out to people she thought she saw in the fields that she made of the hallway. Every now and then, though, she would be found in the kitchen, among a pile of bowls and pots, the tools of her trade when she first came to America. If she remembered nothing else, if she forgot my mother's name or where she was, my grandmother could still pull out a recipe. This is one she often made.

Single 9-inch Butter and Lard Crust (page 25), unbaked

Filling:
1 cup milk
2 large eggs, separated
1 teaspoon unsalted butter, melted
½ cup plus 2 tablespoons sugar
4 Granny Smith apples, peeled, cored, and finely grated
Ground nutmeg to taste

1. Preheat the oven to 325°F.

2. Prepare the crust and set aside in the refrigerator while you make the filling.

3. In a large bowl, using an electric mixer, beat together the milk, egg yolks, butter, and ½ cup of the sugar until thick and pale in color. Stir in the apples and nutmeg.

Pour into the prepared pie pan and bake in the center of the oven for 25 to 30 minutes or until a knife inserted in the middle comes out clean. Cool on a wire rack.

4. Raise the oven to 425°F.

5. In a medium bowl, using an electric mixer, beat the reserved egg whites until stiff peaks form. Add the remaining 2 tablespoons sugar and continue beating until the sugar is well incorporated. Spoon the meringue over the custard, mounding to the center and spreading out to the edges. Bake in the center of the oven for 5 minutes or until the peaks are golden brown.

SERVES 6.

A Word About Apples

*H*enry Ward Beecher strongly advocated the Spitzenburg apple for pies ("Who would put into a pie any apple but?" he asked). I'm not familiar with this variety, nor do I have a strong opinion about what kind to use. Instead I have a strong opinion about what kind NOT to use. Never, unless you're hard up, go to the trouble to make an apple pie with Delicious apples (red or golden, though golden are marginally better than red). McIntoshes are mealy, but if you add just one to other varieties that have a better taste and consistency, a McIntosh can help to deepen the overall flavor.

Unfortunately, these are the only two varieties the supermarkets in my area carry, so I have to make a special trip to one of the farmers' markets in the city when I want to make apple pie. There, I store up on Gravensteins, Jonathans, Staymans, and Winesaps. They keep in my cellar for a few weeks as long as I don't tell anyone else they're down there.

Rosy Apple Pie

*T*his is such a beautiful pie when it is sliced. The tapioca and the raspberries join together to make a sauce around the apple slices. Serve warm with good vanilla ice cream.

Double 9-inch Butter and Lard Crust (page 25), unbaked

Filling:
6 or 7 large cooking apples, peeled, cored, and thinly sliced
1 (10-ounce) package frozen raspberries
1 to 2 tablespoons apple cider (optional)
1 cup sugar
2 ½ tablespoons quick-cooking tapioca
1 tablespoon unsalted butter

1. Preheat the oven to 425°F.

2. Prepare the pastry. Line a 9-inch pie pan with half of the pastry and set aside in the refrigerator, along with the unrolled half, while you make the filling.

3. In a medium saucepan over low heat, bring the apples and raspberries to a boil. If the apples aren't juicy enough, add the cider. Remove from the heat, add the sugar, tapioca, and butter and stir to blend and until the butter melts. Cool, stirring occasionally.

4. Pour the filling into the prepared pastry. Roll out the remaining pastry, cut it into strips, and arrange the strips in a lattice or twist pattern across the top.

5. Bake in the center of the oven for 40 to 45 minutes, until the top crust is golden brown. Watch for spills.

SERVES 6.

Cranberry-Applesauce Pie

*T*he taste of this pie is sweetly tart. My mom tells me she used to make it for her bridge parties and all the women liked it. It went particularly well with Manhattan cocktails, she says. I didn't have a Manhattan the last time I served it; it was Thanksgiving and instead of a turkey I cooked a pork roast. The taste of the pie melded beautifully with the rest of the meal.

Single 9-inch Butter and Lard Crust (page 25), baked

Filling:
1³/₄ cups whole cranberry sauce
2¹/₂ cups applesauce
2 tablespoons fresh lemon juice
2 tablespoons sugar
2 teaspoons unflavored gelatin dissolved in ¹/₄ cup hot water
¹/₂ cup heavy cream
¹/₄ teaspoon ground nutmeg, for dusting (optional)

1. Prepare the crust.

2. In a medium bowl, using an electric mixer set on low, beat the cranberry sauce just to break it up. Add the applesauce, lemon juice, and sugar. Beat until smooth. Stir in the gelatin until well mixed.

3. Turn the filling into the prepared pastry shell and refrigerate until it sets, at least 3 hours. Just before serving, whip the cream to stiff peaks and spread over the top of the pie. Dust lightly with nutmeg (if using) and serve.

SERVES 6.

Marlborough Pie

*T*his pie has a pronounced lemony taste that is very refreshing. It may not look it to read the recipe, but once baked, the texture is very similar to a standard apple pie.

Single 9-inch Butter and Lard Crust (page 25), unbaked

Filling:
1 cup unsweetened applesauce (homemade is best)
1 cup sugar
4 large eggs, lightly beaten
3 tablespoons fresh lemon juice
¹/₂ teaspoon freshly grated fresh lemon zest
2 tablespoons unsalted butter, melted

1. Preheat the oven to 450°F.

2. Prepare the crust and set aside in the refrigerator while you make the filling.

3. In a medium bowl, combine the applesauce, sugar, eggs, lemon juice and zest, and butter. Mix well and pour into the prepared shell.

4. Bake for 15 minutes, then reduce the oven to 350°F and bake for 10 to 15 minutes more or until a knife inserted in the center comes out clean. Cool before serving.

SERVES 6.

Tarte Tatin

*T*he first time I made this classic French dessert I had trouble getting it out of the pan. It's supposed to just flip out but mine didn't. I used—and still do—my old black iron frying pan, but my husband had scrubbed it the night before and scoured off all the seasoning. Just make sure your pan is well seasoned and you shouldn't have any trouble at all.

Single recipe Short Crust Pastry dough (page 34), unbaked

Filling:
8 medium-size tart cooking apples, peeled, cored, and thickly sliced
1 cup sugar
Pinch of ground cinnamon
7 tablespoons unsalted butter

1. Prepare the pastry, roll into a single disk, and refrigerate while you make the filling.

2. Preheat the oven to 375°F.

3. In a large bowl, combine the apples with the sugar and cinnamon. Melt the butter in the 9-inch ovenproof skillet you are going to bake the pie in and pour it over the apples. Stir well to mix.

4. Arrange the apples in a single layer in the skillet used to melt the butter. You can be as precise as the French and do it in concentric circles or you can just smooth the apples out with the back of a spoon in a nice American jumble. However you do it, there should be an even layer. Don't mound.

5. Roll out the dough into a circle that is the same diameter as your skillet and lay it gently over the apples. Bake in the center of the oven for 45 minutes or until the pastry is crisp and brown.

6. Remove the skillet from the oven and place it on the stove over medium heat. Cook (remember the hot handle) for about 15 to 20 minutes or until the bottom of the tart caramelizes.

7. To unmold the tart, place a plate over the top of the skillet and flip it over. The tart should come right out.

SERVES 6.

Crazy Crust Apple Pie

*H*ere's one more of those "impossible" recipes that were in vogue in the late sixties and early seventies, pushed into magazines by the Bisquick company. This particular version comes from a cookbook put out by the Felician Sisters of Our Lady of the Angels Convent in Enfield, Connecticut, that a friend retrieved from her grandmother's house. It doesn't use Bisquick but it draws on the same concept. You can substitute fresh apples for the canned ones, but I think you lose the historical significance of the recipe that way.

1 cup sifted all-purpose flour
1 tablespoon sugar
1 teaspoon baking powder
$\frac{1}{2}$ teaspoon salt
1 large egg
$\frac{2}{3}$ cup vegetable shortening
$\frac{3}{4}$ cup water
1 (12-ounce) can apple pie filling
1 tablespoon bottled lemon juice
$\frac{1}{2}$ teaspoon ground cinnamon

1. Preheat the oven to 425°F.

2. In a medium bowl, combine the flour, sugar, baking powder, salt, egg, shortening, and water. Using an electric mixer set at medium speed, beat until smooth and slightly frothy, about 2 minutes. Pour the batter into a lightly greased 9-inch pie pan.

3. In a medium bowl, combine the apple pie filling with the lemon juice and cinnamon. Pour into the center of the batter. **IMPORTANT**: Do not stir together.

4. Bake for 45 to 50 minutes, until the filling is set and a knife inserted in the center of the pie comes out clean.

SERVES 6.

Crusty Apple Dessert

A simple American variation on Tarte Tatin (page 255). The crust has the taste and consistency of a big biscuit.

Crust:
1 large egg, beaten
$\frac{1}{2}$ cup sugar
$\frac{1}{2}$ cup sifted all-purpose flour
$\frac{1}{2}$ teaspoon baking powder
1 tablespoon vegetable oil

Filling:
8 large tart cooking apples, peeled, cored, and thinly sliced
Sugar and ground cinnamon to taste

1. Preheat the oven to 350°F.

2. In a large bowl, combine the egg, sugar, flour, and baking powder. Blend in the oil to form a pastry. Let rest, covered, in the refrigerator while you make the filling.

3. Sprinkle the apples with sugar and cinnamon to taste, then pour them into a lightly greased 9-inch pie pan. Bake in the center of the oven for 15 minutes.

4. Take the dough out of the refrigerator and roll out on a floured surface to fit over the pie pan. Take the apples out of the oven and quickly place the dough over the top. (You don't have to turn the edges under the pan rim; the crust will shrink a bit, but that's okay.) Return the pie pan to the oven and continue to bake for another 30 minutes or until the top is golden brown.

SERVES 6.

Index